STAR

JOURNAL

SELECTED POEMS

PITT POETRY SERIES
ED OCHESTER, EDITOR

STAR

JOURNAL

SELECTED POEMS

CHRISTOPHER BUCKLEY

UNIVERSITY OF PITTSBURGH PRESS

Published by the University of Pittsburgh Press, Pittsburgh, Pa., 15260
Copyright © 2016, Christopher Buckley
All rights reserved
Manufactured in the United States of America
Printed on acid-free paper
10 9 8 7 6 5 4 3 2 1

ISBN 13: 978-0-8229-6430-8
ISBN 10: 0-8229-6430-9

In Memory of Philip Levine, 1928–2015

I just remembered the stars
I love them too
. . .
they are the endlessness of our longing to grasp things
—NAZIM HIKMET

. . . the distant light
of no new star marked me home.
—PHILIP LEVINE

CONTENTS

1979–1997

3   Why I'm in Favor of a Nuclear Freeze
5   Dust Light, Leaves
6   Halley's Comet from the West Coast, March 22, 1986
7   Evening in Santorini
9   Star Journal
13   Prima Facie
15   Midlife
18   Father, 1952
19   There & Then
21   The Presocratic, Surfing, Breathing Cosmology Blues . . .
24   Camino Cielo
26   Sycamore Canyon Nocturne

1998–2006

31   Sleep Walk
33   Opera
35   Vacuum Genesis
37   Astronomy Lesson: At Café Menorca
38   20 Years of Grant Applications & State College Jobs
40   Early Cosmology
42   March 21st & Spring Begins on Benito Juarez's Birthday in Mexico
44   Photograph of Myself—Monastery of Monte Toro Menorca elv. 1,162 ft.
46   Watchful—Es Castell, Menorca
49   Metaphysical Trees
54   To Ernesto Trejo in the Other World
56   Old News: Poem on a Birthday
59   Poem after Lu Yu
60   Philosophical Poem on the Usual Subjects
63   Memory
64   Wooden Boats
66   Loyalty
68   The Uncertainty Principle
71   Photograph of John Berryman on the Back of *Love & Fame*
73   Travel

2007–2014

77	Poverty
79	We Need Philosophers for This?
81	I Too Am Not a Keeper of Sheep: Variation on a Theme by Pessoa
84	Ode to Clouds
86	In Memory of the Winos at the Moreton Bay Fig Tree, Santa Barbara, CA
88	What Einstein Means to Me
90	Scattering My Mother's Ashes: Santa Barabara, CA
91	Theory of Life on Other Worlds: Contemplating Retirement & Social Security Reform at Shore Line Park
93	Looking West from Montecito, Late Afternoon
94	Hemingway y yo
97	Lost Light
99	Drinking Champagne
100	Note to Gerald Stern Too Long for the Postcard
103	White Shirt
106	The Shape of Things
109	Heart Failure
111	Antiques Road Show
112	Poem on a Birthday
114	Metaphysical Poem Ending with That Line from *Dirty Harry*
116	Before Long
120	Late Iberian Manichaeism & the Crisis of Faith
123	Apnea
125	Creedence Clear Water Metaphysical Reflection
128	Slow Learner: In the Garden
131	Acknowledgments

1979–1997

Why I'm in Favor of a Nuclear Freeze

Because we were 18 and still wonderful in our bodies,
because Harry's father owned a ranch and we had
nothing better to do one Saturday, we went hunting
doves among the high oaks and almost wholly quiet air. . . .
Traipsing the hills and deer paths for an hour,
we were ready when the first ones swooped
and we took them down in smoke much like the planes
in the war films of our regimented youth.
                                        Some were dead
and some knocked cold, and because he knew how
and I just couldn't, Harry went to each of them and,
with thumb and forefinger, almost tenderly, squeezed
the last air out of their slight necks.
                                        Our jackets grew
heavy with birds and for a while we sat in the shade
thinking we were someone, talking a bit of girls—
who would "go," who wouldn't, how love would probably
always be beyond our reach . . . We even talked of the nuns
who terrified us with God and damnation. We both recalled
that first prize in art, the one pinned to the cork board
in front of class, was a sweet blond girl's drawing
of the fires and coals, the tortured souls of Purgatory.
Harry said he feared eternity until he was 17, and,
if he ever had kids, the last place they would go would be a
parochial school.
                        On our way to the car, having forgotten
which way the safety was off or on, I accidentally discharged
my borrowed 12 gauge, twice actually—one would have been Harry's
head if he were behind me, the other my foot, inches to the right.
We were almost back when something moved in the raw, dry grass,
and without thinking, and on the first twitch of two tall ears,
we together blew the ever-loving-Jesus out of a jack rabbit
until we couldn't tell fur from dust from blood. . . .
                                        Harry has
a family, two children as lovely as any will ever be—
he hasn't hunted in years . . . and that once was enough for me.
Anymore, a good day offers a moment's praise for the lizards

daring the road I run along, or it offers a dusk in which
yellow meadowlarks scrounge fields in the grey autumn light .
Harry and I are friends now almost 30 years, and the last time
we had dinner, I thought about that rabbit, not the doves
which we swore we would cook and eat, but that rabbit—
why the hell had we killed it so cold-heartedly? And I saw
that it was simply because we had the guns, because we could.

Dust Light, Leaves

Above autumn's burgundy and rust,
beyond the orange groves
chafing and ruddy in the frost,
a cloud lifts into blue . . .
the west goes up all hay-dust, flame,
and the flat land glimmers
out to it on the day-stream—
it is Millet's sky of *The Angelus*,
that nineteenth-century sky
we have only in paintings
and in these few still moments
in their rose and amber rags.
As a child, I remember this . . .
standing on the creek stones,
dusk moving over the fields
like a ship's hull pulling away
with that first sense of loss
and release; I saw it was
all about the beginning of dust
rising into the long sky's seam,
into my own two eyes and hands.
A chalk-white moon overhead
and to the right, umber waves
of sparrows back and through
the empty trees. . . .
Soon, stars will draw analogies
in the dark, but now the world
is simple as the dead leaves
glowing in this late hour,
simple as our desire
to rise lucent as clouds
in their camisoles of dust,
the cool air burning through us
over leaves drifting on a pond,
over the last memory
of ourselves looking up,
stunned as carp blinking at the light.

Halley's Comet from the West Coast, March, 22, 1986

for Victor Kogler

From the promontory we could hear the dark
arrhythmic break of waves drum the silence
of the early air—then the oil platforms
like an armada, lit and busy in the bay.
We expected every light, all life to be down,
but even this sleepy town did not completely
sleep. Nevertheless, we held out our arms
and measured our blind palms against a gone
horizon line—two up and five to the right—
and there fished about with the naked eye,
halfway down from Mars, for that motionless,
white swish of dust . . . Nothing.
We stood there momentarily stunned
by the light-tide of the Milky Way—that still spin
and irrepressible smudge of its flung grains—
and tried then to pinpoint the stars shifting coolly
to hang there with the thread and bones of all our myths.
We went to binoculars, seining below that lake
of light and caught it there streaming away
in its own bright floss, sinking in the slowed
motion of space like an Independence Day sparkler
in a smoky night's display, deep and south
of wherever it is we are.   My friend recalled
the only time he saw such a wonder was 1956,
his mother rallying the family at 3 a.m. onto
their lawn in the flat heart of San Fernando—
and from there they could see plain as day,
and without binoculars, a raw flash and radiance
surge all the way from the Nevada Test Site,
cannonball across the western night, and then
pulse out.

Evening in Santorini

Above here, there must be a swath of souls
wide and invisibly blue as this water,
and at evening I think they must drift through
the soft pinks and ambers of light,
still dreaming, and confuse their lives
with this one, as if some ash were still
swimming in the violet arc and afterglow—

for again, after dinner and the delicate,
straw colored wine, twilight thickens,
falls and filters out as auburn
as the skin of deer and fisherboys
Minoans left in frescoes on the walls.

Then, the dim taverna sparks with something
like clarinets and mandolins, an old melody
resonant and tenuous as joy; then the few birds
make no excuse for abandoning the trees,
and the young in one another's arms
take slight notice of this rich failing
of the light, or the old turning home in it
from the stony fields, hunkered from cutting
the clear grapes grown low and away from wind.

And once more I dreamed my body floating
hawk-like in its ease above the agate shores,
banking on thin air as the horizon roiled
in flame at the ocean's far end.
                                        But when
you gaze up the sheer and volcanic cliffs
to villages ridged on the crater's lip
they seem no more than snow at an unknown height,
and a switchback toward them from the harbor
spirals like Dante's 50 rings, a whirlwind
of dust smoking upward from the quarried sand—
and so these are the candle ends of the lost
Atlantis and the first world, a legion of dead

vaguely shining beyond any dead we know,
these winding walls and cave-like homes
brushed with clouds and keeping their secrets
as they ascend hand over hand up the air.

Yet, if you climb the one plateau you'll see
them, white as sea foam, wash away into a curve
of blue which rises to the bluer sky for stars
that spill out and glimmer back and forth between
the surface here and whatever surface there.

Star Journal

Astronomy is for the soul—
                      the truth about what
                                    and who we are
                                            and will be.
The universe grinding blithely away
                            and we, reflective grist, stellar pollen
cooling down enough to finally shine—
                            a caucus of dust and acids blown
over the warped table of space,
                      arriving on the shirttails of comets to lap down
on tundra, settle on palmetto leaves,
                            blinking above an isthmus white with sand. . . .
                              *
And so unconsciously we take our breath
                                    into orbit about the solar apparatus
of the heart—
                  star with its own fusion and collapse—each measure and molecule
voluble but
                  unaccountable in a code
                                    comprising even the weightless freight
of thought
                  as we stand out each night exhaling
                                          dim clouds from the ghosted
wing-span of our lungs. . . .
                              *
We have built machines
                      that can see light burning
                                          from the lost beginning—
faint quasars, a print-out just coming
                                    through the hazed background buzz
after fifteen billion years.
                              *
From our vantage point in the outer precincts,
                                    we tune in radio from the first
broadcast, big downbeat still on every network
                                    and starry frequency

as we go for a spin through the galactic plasma,

                      a kind of Dynaflow along

the boulevards,

         oxbows and sluice gates of time. . . .

*

Telescopes *are* time machines,

            lanes for recovered light

                    bringing the past

up to speed, pulling down the crystal spheres

                and broken symmetries,

exposing our surroundings,

         our irrepressible, elemental histories

                with which

we continue

      to negotiate as if the wheel were firmly in our hands.

*

Space itself is slipping away,

        expanding,

          but into what?

              Aristarchus of Samos,

against Ptolemy and the popular astrophysics,

          deduced that earth was a planet,

that stars were very far away indeed!

        A little over 2,000 years,

            and his information

was confirmed.

       Still, there is the black frame of space,

           stars untrue

in our parallax view—their bent scintillations so many

          curve balls breaking

over the outside corner of the plate.

           And so our doubt about everything

published above us in the dark,

        and then the blank and sweeping margins

of the east each dawn

        after we've again tried to decipher the shorthand

in the night.
                    Sitting up at dawn, starlings appear across the lawn
like black holes
                    in the mist-bright sheen.
                                        Birds congregate, begin a capella—
cavatinas and recitatives— without the least introspection,
                                        time management
or stress . . . neither do they sew.
                    A steady disregard of the attrition of air,
the ambiguous blue going of the world—
                                        something like a rose-colored nebula
boiling in their breasts, moving them
                    to praise to matter the implications,
the copyright of the cold.

                              *

The lawn sprinklers whirl out their silver
                                        and unerring loops . . . gravity keeping us
here—the weak force and the strong,
                              the invisible and the dissembled something
in the unified field
                    even as light is fused and driven through
                                        charged tines of air,
torching the tree, black Y against
                              the mustard sky, wringing out the horizon,
an ash of arms extending, funnel cloud
                              taking farm house and Ford Galaxy sedan
up the violet ascension of the sky,
                              against gravity and half the Midwest
on the TV A.M. News, particles accelerated,
                              snowy dots of channels flipped through.
Out the window, the glitter
                    in the night river washed away, discord of black
sand rolling over some last bright bones,
                              wing bones, let's say, holding it all up
about us as we reel outward,
                    carrying our blue and parochial atmosphere
with us, our little argument advanced

                              against all the blind stuff of space,
the dark matter now 95% of everything,
                              denser than anthracite with time,
dead energy so massed it will never shine
                              nor harbor one mote of mica,
one iced diamond-fleck not inked and unknowable.
                                        Only the fingerprints,
the gravitational arcs hold
                    the pearl-like and whirling Milky Way in thrall,
keep the arms swirled,
                    brilliantly together, rotating in sync with
the yolky center, edges bright
                    with the hum and singing of atoms swimming
outward, burning away
                    somewhere nothing ends.

Prima Facie

I've always liked the story of Bertrand Russell
giving a public lecture on astronomy,
and a woman standing up afterwards to say
it was all rubbish, that the earth was really flat
and supported on the back of a giant tortoise!
And when Russell asked just what the turtle was standing on,
the woman was ready and replied, "Why, it's turtles
all the way down."
                    Doesn't it add up this flawlessly
while we take our short swim off these rocks—
stunned in the immediate and febrile good will
of the light as it replays every summer
traveling home from the shore, green sea
still sparkling in our veins, horizon's blue frame
holding, crepuscular, one star only burning
there and inside of us in continuous disputation
of the dark. . . .
                    And again this evening I'm watching
a feckless delegation of clouds depart for home
or perhaps the rain-emptied coast of Dieppe, I'm brooding
on immortality where white sandwich wrappers
lifted above those chalk-dull cliffs, where seagulls argued
low along a flinty sea blown back along the quai
as if there were another element to the light that we,
stalled there and as simple as those wind-thinned trees,
were letting slip away. . . .
                    A circus had cleared off
overnight, and papers scuttled on the long green field,
a red-and-yellow poster waving from a bench, were little
to say time and space had been put to use there and then,
and in that way—unremarkable now and shuffling off
with the salt shifting of the air.
                    A wafer of sun
cut across the clouds' grey scroll, the black edges
of night bleeding in until bright specks floated up
on the blank plate of space with all our unsupported
paradigms for science and for art—the dark ocean

spattered with refracted light like the grainy surface
of the soul—both perhaps expanding, still being etched
with the lost music of the spheres—while we were only
at sea again in our heart, pointing out first-hand the old
shapes and overlappings, the sure and selfsame stars.

Midlife

Because out of nowhere one day
the grace disappeared
from my body, rarely to be seen
again except in that unconscious
wrist-snap of a racket head as it kicks out
the side-ways arc of an American twist,
I went out for my birthday and, instead
of a *Cos d'Estournel* '82, bought
two Day-Glo green-and-yellow parakeets,
some seed, cuttle bone, and cage,
along with a flagon of something
truly unremarkable from Czechoslovakia.

We carried them finger to cage,
these frank dispositions, attended
as an inflated chatter proclaimed
their vibrant devotion to the air.
We spoke to them much as if they were
autistic children, capable somehow
of one spectacular, clear feat—as if,
being simple, they were simply loved—
as if, perhaps, they might take the place
of children, had one wanted children. . . .

                    *

And this year, players in the Series
looked younger than ever before, all of them—
even stodgy catchers who hadn't shaved.
And never have I been so attentive to weather—
where the jet stream might drag down the clouds,
road ice, airport delays as if there were something
to be done. I especially enjoy the channel that shows
temperatures in Barcelona or in Rome
superimposed on postcard vistas
so starched with sunlight that when
I close my eyes I'm walking the *Ramblas*
or the *Corso*, or off praising one tree or another
in the *Jardin des Plantes*. Or I see the supple lace

of jacarandas, the deep-iris sky over Montecito—
my legs were somehow then attached
to the tireless direction of the breeze,
as unconcerned as the itinerant clouds.

Now I notice most my friends
have rowing machines or stationary bikes,
and I have bought a fancy one on time,
the kind with a dashboard of lights and beeps
like a starship, one with a computer read-out
for hills, levels, duration, intensity, RPMs.
It's called a Life Cycle, and not a minute goes by
that the irony is lost on me. It's the kind
I used to warm up on in the mirrored gym
before running or workouts on the weight machines—
but lately I walk by refusing
to even glance at it, hamstrung
by a flagging affinity for pain.

Nonetheless, I have not taken to
wearing a cardigan or bow tie,
nor have I insisted students
call me Dr. or Professor, this or that....
Because next year, when I get my grant,
I'm heading for the coast and home—
going to buy one of those old big boards and,
without one thought for carcinoma,
stay all day long in the surf, nose-riding,
shooting the curl on shoulder-high sets
like nobody's business. And on Fridays
I'm going to hit an Italian restaurant
I know and eat rigatoni like Tony Quinn
in that old Fellini film, drink a few
water glasses of red wine with friends
and walk out late into starlight, into the blue
and immutable sea sounds of the past.

And nowadays, more and more in dreams
I'm flying—just taking off from the sidewalk
mid-conversation, pushing the air back like water
with my hands, the way I remember learning
to dog paddle in the Pacific, bobbing then
above the azure levels in the world.
It's simple, something I always knew,
but something larger, more elementary
than all the images of parochial school,
something hidden like the white and floating
hearts of saints, something I had just forgotten
all this time—a little transcendental muscle gone soft
but coming back, some instant weight-loss plan.
I rise then effortlessly above the cypress
and eucalyptus trees, and there I am, suddenly
once more gliding over that sea cliff and the coast
for as long as I can remember. . . .

Father, 1952

He must be 30 or 31,
and the brown autumn light is dying
in the tops of jacarandas lining Anacapa Street.
He's just picked me up from school
on the big hill in back of town, and,
riding in our station wagon's wide front seat,
the whole windshield is a field of blue
filled with sea, and a sky bending to meet it
where the earth curves miles out in air. . . .
I'm looking up after unlacing my school shoes
and pulling on cowboy boots, black ones
with white and gold lilies blossoming at the tops—
this is not that long ago. . . .
                      Forty years,
and it all comes back the day I bend down
to try on a pair of wingtips, and there he is
in his camel hair sport coat and green knit tie.
His black and wavy hair blows again in the wind
from the open window of the car—again,
we're taking the curves above the Mission,
the limestone walls and pepper trees aflame
along the road, and in that last blindness of sun,
the mackerel clouds, the clusters of pepper pods
burn red as the bell-tower domes. . . .
I'm staring into the light spread thick as sawdust
across the windshield. With his college ring
he's tapping out a tune on the steering wheel,
stubbing a Philip Morris. Now he's whistling,
it's 4:30, and the daylight behind us is going
violet on the mountain range. I'm content
in my boots, standing on the green vinyl seat
to see above the dash—below, a harbor mist
rolls in beneath the yellow nettle of stars,
the Xs of seagulls' wings marking their places
as they drift slowly before the dark. I'm looking left,
into the purple sky—we're coasting down
a last silent hill. Nothing, I think, has happened
in our lives—he's happy—this is not that long ago. . . .

There & Then

Though there's no going back
it happens all the time—sleep or day-dreams,
and I'm on the corner of State and Micheltorena,
noon on a Saturday, the wide sidewalks shimmering
with mica, Simonized Chryslers and Oldsmobiles, women
with coral or ivory shopping bags sauntering in and out of I. Magnin,
Lou Rose, as I wait for Fowler, Cooney, and Schneider, the station wagons
that will let them out and leave us on our own in all the world we know, seaside
among white stucco and red tile roofs, a little principality of blue air and sun where
someone with a dollar in change is free. Flipping 50¢ pieces, we strut with confidence
into Woolworth's for M&Ms weighted-out by the pound and then head down to the California
Theater on Canon Perdido, the last place where, sill under 12, you get in for 15¢. No loges,
a descending center aisle, and we sit in the cave-like glow, in 1959 content to know almost
nothing about our lives or what we're about to see despite a newsreel and our first year
of Social studies. We're happy, our high-top sneakers squeaking on the sticky floor,
the freight of sugar so thoroughly embalming our veins that we're fairly oblivious
to whatever Robert Mitchum and Yvonne De Carlo, Mel Ferrer and Joan Fontaine
are up to. We're supposed to be at the Arlington for cartoons, Audie Murphy
and John Wayne, World War II again, where one dollar leaves us barely
enough for Jujyfruits or Junior Mints. So we opt for black & white,
the burning silver profiles when someone's kissed. We can't tell
film noir from adult romance, but guess what we see goes on
somewhere in the world, though no one we know drinks
martinis, flies to Mexico or Singapore. Four hours with
previews and intermission—we exit walking slowly
up the ramp in the building's shade before
stepping out, almost blinded by the slant
of winter light sharp as tin foil
as we shield our eyes.
Next year, it's 50¢ for everyone
and we'll go there only one more time
for *Alexander the Great* starring Richard Burton
something we think we'll understand—the spectacle and bloody Technicolor war.
And though Alexander dies reasonably young at 32, that point in time floats out
further than the ancient past. The rainbow of neon tubes hums on, the marquee
fizzes and pops in the 5:00 dusk as I'm the last one to be picked up. When the doors
close for good, I'll remember little about that battle for the civilized world raging

all afternoon—I'll recall instead the face of Kim Novak, tragic and blond in a love scene as Kirk Douglas walked out on her a year or so before, and there and then think I know the complete depth and extent of loss, coming soon, out of the dark.

The Presocratic, Surfing, Breathing Cosmology Blues . . .

When the great waters went everywhere, holding the germ, and generating lights,
Then there arose from them the breath of the gods.
                    — *"Hymn to the Unknown God" from the* Rig Veda

Let's get real gone.
                    —*Elvis Presley*

The idea of an infinite number of stars brought Newton to his knees, for that would turn
    the sky into a blazing haze—flame rises naturally—and so reasoned Empedocles
        Homer, and Anaxagoras who filled the farthest reaches with fiery light. . . .

The back pages of cosmic history blow open, a bright litter of particles swimming in
    the blue backwash of quasars, kernels back at the beginning smoldering finally
        through to us now, telescopes probing not just into space
            but into time. . . .

So galaxies in the Coma Cluster appear to us as they looked seven hundred million years
    ago, about the time the first jellyfish—its own roseate nucleus of cells and
        spinning arms—was developing on earth,

where, some years later, I would turn up at 9, walking tip toe along Miramar Beach,
    avoiding the pink and scattered nebulae washed up for a mile around—
        a sting like hot coals, a cold quivering mass of burning stars.

Or where I sit now, admiring a sugar maple, flag of impending flame, angelic breathing
    we attribute to trees as we bivouac at the perimeter of nothing as instrumental
        as beauty, and are mainly recursive, among other elemental things.

What wouldn't it be worth to have time again to worry about incursions of fog over
    the blacktop, the starry orange groves dissolving on the slow drive to school,
        to worry about the spelling of grey or gray, or Mississippi, the mysterious
            lives of Saints, a laundry line of levitating miracles commemorated
                along the church's tomb-dark walls

where beeswax candles, placed cross-wise on my throat, would save me from choking
    on the bones of fish, and holy water sprinkled along the air keep a sea-wide
        iniquity from seeping under the closed door of the soul so I might be
            admitted to the beatific company of clouds, the clear apertures
                in an updraft of wind.

And I in fact sometimes pondered the unsubstantiated Soul—invisible, but something
just the same—like a glass of water filled to different levels during music class,
sounding a high or low note as a finger orbited the transparent rim.

Or in back bookcases, The World Book Encyclopedia, all the blank space edging dark
columns of letters proclaiming the Hittites' fierce knowledge of iron, the Code
of Hammurabi, The Lighthouse at Pharos, and the first space capsule
burning like a thimble of coal in the stratosphere.

Yet, when we think about it, our youth lasts all our lives, trailing us like a comet tail of ice
and dust, or the way angels, like knots in a rope of light, are still let down to us
from the dark in Caravaggio's first "St. Matthew," the one sent up
in flames in the bombing of Berlin

whose atoms are still associated in the grey haze that constantly resettles that sky, re-
claiming its dust in the thin half-light of loss, in the past riding that freight
of light out to a universe where all things are contingent upon each other,
upon, as Anaximander had it, "The Indefinite."

There's much that matters in that dark where my hands are full of the brilliant dross
off the recent edge of discovery, data no one in school had the least idea existed
when I took my D in General Science.

Now I'm writing it all down—Vacuum Genesis, Lookback Time—thinking I'm getting
somewhere, only to realize I need another course in Italian Cinema just to
make the metaphors make sense!

Was it Luchino Visconti's *Death in Venice* or Vitorio De Sica's *Brief Vacation?* Dirk
Bogarde on the Lido coughing out the dark matter of his lungs for some
blond boy in a bathing suit as Mahler's symphony moved like a cloud
of melting glass over the sea,

or that beaten angel of a housewife escaping her truck driving, mule-headed husband
in Torino with black stars on her X-rays, a silt of light slowing in her veins
which took her up to the state sanitarium in the snowy Alps, a comet-quick
brush with a younger man reconstituting the rose-colored clouds
of her lungs, but sending her finally back?

And I remember holding my breath, the universe expanding inside my lungs as I was
tumbled like a rag in the spin-cycle of ten foot surf a quarter mile off shore,
riding the point break at Rincon and plunged into the white salt-roar
of froth, my chest burning as I shot up to that heaven

of air above the surface—and while heaven could, in theory, have been anywhere,
    it was there that minute as I swallowed the air's cool light, mindless of every
        molecule and the constant state of flux all things are in.

And regardless of the frenzy of atoms and the sub-atomic voids, I'd have sold my soul
    for my dinged-up plank, anything to hold to and fill my flattened pipes
        before the next wave with its five feet of churning soup rolled in,
            beneath which I'd have to dive, count ten, and come up again
                gasping toward a low tide of rocks.

In college, staring out past the spires of Italian cypress, wind bending the invisible
    blue beyond the second story classroom windows, the thick glass sinking,
        soaked with old light, the Presocratics were proclaiming the single source
            to everything. Half conscious, at swim in the 60s, I was reaching
                for the first idea that would keep my head above dark waters.

And, like Einstein, whom I hadn't read, I didn't bother about the details and showing
    my work—all the math and elegant equations—I just wanted to know what was
        on God's mind when he shook up this *boule de neige* and let time-space
            float out and gather here with our little neighborhood of
                respiration and recourse to nothing but light?

Camino Cielo

Santa Barbara, California

Heaven's way, lost
river of breath, this *road*
to the sky running out
along the Santa Ynez.
I'm driving the mountain crest
toward a stand of cloud-shaped trees;
one remove from the world,
the delays of light
up from the sea,
a skein of salt blistering
ironwood and manzanita.

Dragon flies cut and hum,
iridescent as gasoline, as new leaves
along the green and sunset flames.
And against the evening gloss,
jays are dark as quasars,
that deep, first-ever blue
burning through to us
after fifteen billion years—
and this is, for a moment,
a place where all the past
has gone.
       Forty years ago
my father built his tower
back here on Broadcast Peak,
and with 100,000 watts proclaimed
the power and extent of "easy listening."
He took in the vista, had his vision—
the business of this world was business;
confidence and a pressed gabardine
were all that were required for the keys
of commercial kingdoms to fall
into your hands.
       And though he stood
on this promontory in the sun's salt-haze,

looked to the windward or the lee,
he was no Balboa, and discovered little
more than men before him who
embraced the gold starred surface
of the sea. All those years
he never heard the dark ledgers
thudding shut in the small rooms
of the blood.

              But his music is still
on the air, his radio tower pressing
sentimentally into the valley winds,
the cross-braces pitted with stars
of rust. All of it simply outlasting him
and the brief illusion
that wherever it is we are,
we spin essentially at the center
of the spheres.

              But only
the raptors ride up here
as thermals build, etching circles
in the sky, an eye on everything
humming blood-wise in their sight.
The sage, and purple thistle, paint brush
like blood flecks vibrating on a breeze—
dusk thumbing the center of each
wind-blown bloom.

              Below, the city
shines with the emerald precisions
of pools, a pewter light glistens
off jacarandas and Alexandra palms,
the Pacific stretching away
on the insubstantial promise
of the air.

Sycamore Canyon Nocturne

> But home is the form of the dream, & not the dream.
>
> —*Larry Levis*

Home again in dreams, I'm walking that foothill road
as the last morning star slips away over canyon walls—
red-gold riprap of creek rock, ferns splayed in the blue
shade of oaks, the high yellow sycamores, oat straw catching
sun at my feet. Wind-switch, then the chalk-thick stillness
saying angels, who come down here to dip their wings
and give the water its color.
                              Yet even when I'm allowed back
along the weedy path of sleep to this green and singing space,
I know someday air will be set between my shoulder blades
and arms and all my bones, and, little more than clouds,
the clouds will be my final lesson until I'm taken off
into some clearer imagining. . . .
                              In exile, it is hard to love God.
What then, must I renounce? The Psalter of evergreens
ringing along Sheffield drive? The loquat and acacia
burning through ocean fog? Can I speak of love
almost a life ago, syllables repeating the skin's sweet salts
and oils like lemon blossoms riding the August heat?

I love the life slowly taken from me, so obviously spun out
flower-like, and for my own use, it seems, against some future
sky—the world, just a small glory of dust above a field
one autumn afternoon—the resinous pines and a back road
full of birds inside you.
                              What more could wishes be,
who would live there again, sent back among the breathing
acanthus to lift unconsciously with morning and with mist?
I would.
              Moonlight or dreamlight, this is the world, giving
and taking away with the same unseen hand, desires winding
around the soul like fleshy rings on a tree. Where this canyon
levels out, I'd eat the wild sun-red plums, the sweet light
of the juice carrying through me my only hymn.

I know God, old flame wearing through the damp sponge
of the heart, that candle I cannot put out coming back

each time it seems extinguished. And so I must bless everything,
take anything given me—these words, their polish or pity,
the absences they bear like winter trees ascending
the ridge, so many starving angels in the early dusk,
and then the dark, and the broken order of prayer. . . .

I know you are listening. Like the sky. And the birds
going over, aren't they always full of light? But to shine
like these trees again, that air hovering on the canyon walls—
sometimes, all I want to be is the dreaming world.

1998–2006

Sleep Walk

Fourteen and I knew from nothing—
but there I was in the darkened gym
to get some idea. Someone was stacking the 45's
and my friend Carlson was doing The Stroll
with Maryann Garland, gliding around the corners
of the basketball court with that strut, scuff, and easy slide.
I knew Surf Music and Motown cold, but even if
I worked up nerve to ask a girl to dance, there was no way
when it came to the Stomp, the Mash Potato,
those spins, dips, and twists kids were pulling off
like varieties of religious experience.

As recently as 8th grade, in classes the nuns
roped us into after school, I had only managed
a reluctant fox trot, as if I were dragging my shoes
through a dance floor of fudge. And those meager skills
had only lead to heartbreak and Virginia Cortez,
the dark stars of her eyes burning through me
at a party where parents drank coffee in the kitchen
and came out every quarter hour to keep lights on
in the living room. She leaned her head into my shoulder
and shorted out the entire network of circuits
in my skin—and though we barely moved across
the carpet to the Statues and "Blue Velvet," sparks
stung our hands and pulled us into a world where
you could get lost in no time. . . .
                                    So there I was, fourteen
and through with love, putting on my best Bob Mitchum
tough-guy face, saying I'd seen it all already, and so what?
But someone switched the disks to Doo Wop, the Flamingos
and slow oldies, and the whole floor of dancers froze,
swaying only a fraction to "In The Still of The Night"
before Santo & Johnny's "Sleep Walk"
ground any pretense of movement to a halt
with its bone-deep bass laying down a line of hormones
like an infection in the blood—the high, sliding lead
seeming to lift all the sighing dreamers

out the transoms of the gym into the starlight spinning
through the blue spring night.
                              I'd been watching a couple
in the middle—the girl, a pageboy blond, all curves
in a cotton dress, and a tall guy from the team—seniors
who'd been melting into each other all evening,
enough steam rising there to press a dozen shirts.
Both her arms hung on his neck, his arms wound around
her waist—as hot as it then got before you were thrown out
and called into the office during home room on Monday.
What wouldn't I give to be them in that dim light
and crepe paper, all confidence and careless in love?

But I knew from nothing—no one told me to be careful
what you wish for. And two and a half years turned me
loose in that exact spot, arms around Kathy Quigley,
eyes closed, feet stuck to the gym floor and "Sleep Walk"
stringing out a last legitimate embrace. It was time to walk out
those double metal doors, rubbing our eyes, dizzy
with our own tranced blood buzzing in the dark.
We had to kiss quickly so she could get home by 12:00—
the world still that careful and slow.
                              I'd drive around
for an hour, up and down State, pull into Petersons for a shake,
circle the town, radio off, cruising with the windows down,
with that twang and ground swell bass from Santo & Johnny
still pulsing in my head, sure this was everything there was
despite college coming, and the war. I looked up into the night
where the stars slurred like the notes in that song
and wished again, as if I knew what I wanted. . . .

Opera

for Bill Matthews

Upgraded from economy class, I'm flying down the freeway
feeling rich as God, behind the wheel of a silver, full-size sedan—
quad stereo, cruise control, gold glowing digital clock—
and for a minute I think of that article on the Sultan of Brunei
checking out from a hotel and leaving enough money in tips
to fund disease research for a year. But soon I'm satisfied
just floating through a corridor of pines, popping in my tape
of Carerras, Domingo, and Pavarotti. A chorus of blue above me,
a few arpeggios of clouds to the right, not unlike the sky
over the Baths of Caracalla where they're singing—three ancient
stories of brick still standing on the edge of Rome. We came
across it one summer as workers were erecting the stage
and high dusty towers for *Aida*—40 then, and just beginning
to listen. . . .
            70 mph and I'm transported by the wind-swell
of the orchestra, lifted by the violins, brought back to earth
by violoncellos, the heart still climbing that white ladder of hope
with *Rondine al Nido*, Pavarotti's power surge spiking current
along my arms. I let the tape rewind—this is serious, I keep hearing,
we are all going to die, hopelessly though, and at last in love
with the world. By now, most my aspirations let go, blown by me
like litter along the road, I'm just happy to be breathing, to be soaring
in such company, to have a heart thumping its own sprung notes.

No one is going to sleep until Pavarotti has an answer
to the riddle and claims the starry heart of *Turandot*—now all three
encore *Nessun Dorma*, and in the bridge all the angels sing,
sodality in the last movement of lost air. I too want to fly,
to know the ineluctable extravagance of the spirit
about to slip out of the tux, beyond the fingertips
into the night sky.
            But I have to rent a car to hear
these tapes punched up to the proper brick-shaking valence.
I have to leave town, get away from young friends at parties
where the angels all wear red shoes, where I'm told Dwight Yoakam
is "Bakersfield Opera," where CDs are stacked like potato chips—

either trash bands like Pilonidal Cyst, Meat Puppets, and
Mud Honey, or time fractures from the 70s, Hendrix, Led Zeppelin,
and the Chambers Brothers. Nothing close to carrying off the sky
like Verdi or Puccini—in heaven, they have to be cooking Italian!

Friends my age are all listening to opera—Pavarotti's Richter Scale
and range proving there's another level, and though the register,
like the body, is giving way to gravity, there is something
there just above us.
                    The astral body must be like this,
all sentience and incorporeal as sound. I want some singing
about that—all the red and blue bright threads spun out
from our hearts, spooled above the gilt-edged clouds,
above the scraps of flesh and diminuendos of ordinary time.
I want this feeling of atoms falling out of the crystal orbits
of the earth, yet reclaimed by arias, by cavatinas.
Carrerras recovering from cancer, Domingo's good looks
going south, Pavarotti barely able to move—yet each lifting
past the burning limits of the dark. And conducting everything,
Zubin Mehta—surely that has to be an angel's name?
But this is serious we are all going to die.

Vacuum Genesis

If you don't know how you got somewhere you don't know where you are.
—*James Burke*

"A blue-million of 'em" my aunt always said—we were looking up
above Lexington for a meteor shower and saw only the unmitigated
skyline; too much light too close to us, all those electrons going
to town, diffuse between the air around us. I'd seen it once before,

the night full of flares, sparking out of nowhere, vanishing again
into the otherwise empty scope of things. But a vacuum, it turns out,
is never truly empty. Even when the universe was nothing more
than a held breath, a vast lake flat with helium and hydrogen,

it only took a hiccup in that slick molecular mix for every ten billion
quark/anti-quark pairs created and annihilated in that first blast
toward light, to leave one extra quark behind—a tiny surplus—all
that was required to evolve the chain link clusters and whirligigs

we point to today. Apparently something can emerge from nothing—
virtual particles buzz like halos around real ones, and that pretty much
accounts for biological creatures like ourselves who look up and petition
the pinpoint night, who find at our fingertips language for that dimension-

less place, name animals and plants, the spins on sub-atomic particles,
their "flavors"—*Strange and Charmed*. Untied from the unities and set
stumbling about, we arrived at parallel universes—on the bubble, stacked up,
bottled, bright ships on a black expanding shelf, not a supporting speck

of evidence for something that may or may not be there, wherever
"there" might be. We had a ranch house on the coast, a yard burning
with wild nasturtiums, clusters of blue pines, and periwinkle,
and a station wagon on time which let us slip unnoticed through

the streets of suburbia, no one imagining mother and I sharing
a can of tomato soup with fried bologna on wheat all those nights
father was working late. We sat in the kitchen, the GE radio—
purple, plastic, the size of a bread box—on the table. Its one clock-like

dial coaxed in music always less interesting than the warped tones
and oscillations I found flipping between stations. I pulled in the blank
imponderable sounds of space and peeked through the hundred holes
in the Masonite backing to the tubes—orange filaments glowing

beneath their dusk-dark caps like the tails of comets—and each night
hadn't the least idea where it all was headed. Soon enough, TVs appeared,
and by the end of the fifties the future was clear in a set whose mahogany
cabinet doors opened to *Buck Rogers*, *Rocky and the Space Pirates*,

or Saturday mornings of posses and bandidos, six-shooters firing
all over Malibu or Chatsworth, and tree-thick back lots of L.A., glorious
in black & white where heroes galloped off over the sunset hills and
disappeared in a cloud of dust. After staring at a bombardment of electrons

all morning, I was sent out to play in our wide neighborhood, the boundaries
of which I knew well. I was tethered to the daylight's long string unraveling
from all that vacant and unquestioned space beyond our drive, and charged
only to find my way home before the first star appeared again in the sky.

Astronomy Lesson: At Café Menorca

I have just asked for stars—and wine from a region
where grapes are not clustered in remorse. I want to speak
     as elegantly as the sun-struck sentences of fish shifting
in the cove, but here I sit in my coat, crumpled and mute
     as a cloud—old troubles traveling the small distances of salt
and pepper, elbows alone eloquent with the shine of tables,
     acknowledged by dust from one establishment to the next
as I point skyward at the fiery crests of local birds.
     Aqui estan las estrellas Señor. And a plate is set before me
with pastries and crème caramels, a spiral galaxy sugared
     with light. *Pero, estoy triste*—I cannot recall the words
for light, for clouds, cannot place an order for rain
     deep and green as under the trees of childhood, or for a sky—
el cielo—reflecting both faces of the sea—*blanco y azul*—
     or for the first planets white as soap flakes above the bay.
Algo Mas Señor? Something stronger perhaps? I try again
     asking for brandy, one with the courage of fire, and a *café
con limòn,* without the rind of laughter that edges the dark.
     Es mas tarde—es todo Señor? No, I'd also like the glass wrapper
my heart arrived in from the sky, and add whatever advice
     the wind can offer on living far from home. *Por favor, Señor,
es mas tarde,* the help is sad—even the stars here are overworked.

20 Years of Grant Applications & State College Jobs

"Why, without theory there is no meaning. "

—former colleague at a department meeting

All I want now is a small dirt patio beneath two or three pines,
maybe one palm glittering with dates, one lemon sapling in a terra-cotta pot
standing for hope. A place where I can return to my scholarship of the sky,
re-establish a franchise with the sun. A place—I swear—where I will leave
most of the talking to the trees and purple finches, where I am at last renowned
among sparrows for my philosophy of crumbs.
                                                A place where I walk out
each day at 8:00 or 9:00 to appraise the likelihood of daylight advancing
beyond the cool green efforts of the boughs, where I set my coffee
and unread newspaper down on the metal table—a round one, the size
of a trash can lid, just big enough for wine and glasses, a basket of bread—
one painted that thick civic green like those in the sidewalk cafes
and parks in Paris—my last concession to a sentimental education.

I won't mind that the paint's chipped or that salt air eats away the legs;
I will praise the fog, its long beggar's coat dragging in from Point Conception
like some lost uncle in an Ingmar Bergman film. I will praise the tiny ranch-
style house the color of fog, my luck to end up in Lompoc, the last place
on the California coast almost no one wanted. I will refold the paper,
my notes scrawled in the margins where I've tried again to locate
the trace elements of God.
                                To feel industrious, I'll get to my feet
about 11:00 and spray the hose around to keep down the dust—
a bit extra for the lantana lining the flagstones to the door,
a bit more for the aloe vera, the pomegranate, their blossoms aflame.
Every so often, I'll rake the patches of pine needles into a pile,
but before I decide where to move them next, a gust rearranges them
with an abstract but even hand.
                                What will I care,
sitting in my rain bleached chair, one leg tapping the shade, the other
going to sleep in the sun, content to stare at my hot-pink hibiscus
slowly ascending the stucco wall? After 20 years, what can it matter
how long it takes to burn its way up the glistening air?
Even the stars are wearing down without a thought for us,
unattainable all this time. That should have been a lesson long ago. . . .

I hereby resign all pretenses to the astronomy of New York—
appointments, invitations, awards, the genius grants.
Whenever the phone doesn't ring, it's them.
I'll settle for this wooden gate, a gravel drive announcing friends
who arrive for walks, for the Zinfandel and dish of Spanish olives;
friends who remember the sea, how good it was 20 years ago,
loose as driftwood in our lives, to have nothing and happily
drink that green, hard Chablis each evening by the Pacific
thinking we would have that light.
                                    Now, I love the grey
and ragtag gulls whose hoots and aggravation betray their finds—
all that chance deserves. So after our walk, we're satisfied
just sitting outside, a Pavarotti aria holding off death,
drifting out the kitchen window onto the ambered light.

And what can we make of the Maya now? Their lost tongue,
their psalms of stone? They disappeared in the middle
of setting it all down and no one missed them for centuries.
And what was behind the anonymous workers of the Nazca Plains,
scraping off the desert's scrofulous skin for images of animals
and some politico's son, lines so long they only make sense from the sky—
and none of us birds?
                                    Whose administrative mission was that?
100 years and the job will still be there. How good now to say Good-bye
 to that arrogance which asks if there can be meaning
without first arranging the padded folding chairs of theory.

I'd like to apply for my life. I want the Guggenheim
to give me back my good will, the ease—no, the joy—
I once carried around with me, going down the street
in uncertainty, not enough gas in the tank to get out of town.
But I'll settle for this unpopular valley of fog, cholla flats and sand,
the occasional breeze thumbing my book, humming a blue line.
I'll take a small patio of unglamorous old dirt, a few pines
speaking simply in the resinous language of the only world
there is, immediate and meaningful as your next breath.
I'll praise the uneventful afternoon, and accept the wind
applauding in the silver dollar eucalyptus as my reward.

Early Cosmology

Where am I when I first hear the high orbiting
harmony of April Stevens and Nino Tempo's
"Deep Purple," or the Marcels' doo-wopped
"Blue Moon" nonsense circling the lyrics of love,
reverberated on KIST's Top 40?
                                    Somewhere
unknown on night-wide State Street,
submerged in that boat of a Belair, cruising
forever on a dollar-fifty's worth of gas,
tuning in each *bomp bomp-bomp-bomp,*
ba bomp ba bomp bomp, da dip da dip-dip,
thinking . . . God knows what
I was thinking—the charged gloss
of street lights rebounding off the chrome
buttons of the radio—all that electricity
spinning off into the everlasting sky.

Kathy Young & The Innocents swirled
"A Thousand Stars" through bad speakers
in a rust-bucket Chevrolet—a six-pack
in the trunk, and a misery mute enough
on the side streets as I turned up the tunes
and took in the salt air's intoxication
as if I understood the mind's invisible
source of light, and from where in the under-
elaborated heavens it was likely to break clear.

And just for the record, I knew nothing
of Art Rimbaud and his jazz quintet,
who played alto or who tinkled the ivories
to "I Left My Love In Babylon"—never knew
who slipped out of Toledo and threw
that cymbal shining like the rings
of Saturn from the window of the Merc,
the radio slurring "Stardust."
                                    Whatever

I knew, I picked up later, commercial TV
spanning the prairies; Halo Shampoo
and Old Golds—*A Word From Our Sponsor.*
Coast to coast, Edward R. Murrow
at the center of a solar system of smoke.
Andre Kostelanetz's "Saber Dance"
was the music of the spheres on Ed Sullivan
for some poor soul sweating it out
in a tuxedo and pencil mustache,
frantically balancing dishes on sticks,
running along a table, spinning
another before the first ones
collapsed from orbit like planets
in that wobbly air—father fiddling
with the wiry rabbit ears
when the images went ghostly.
A couple minutes of stage light
and suspended saucers were all
the black & white '50s required.

What chance now someone out there
in the unwavering wherever
will one day care to uncode our beams,
and figure, where, on the background track,
among some stuttering powder-bright stanzas
we ever were?
                    Each night of your remaining
few thousand nights, all those galaxies
and plasma-colored nebulae still
spinning in your head, you walk up
the dark hill from work, looking out
to the Milky Way, the hiss wobbling
in the center of the egg-yolk wheel—
and you retrace every constellation
you know, all the self conscious metaphors
and shapes that confirm nothing more than
what a glimmering plate of dust it all might be.

March 21st & Spring Begins on Benito Juarez's Birthday in Mexico

In Mexico today, Benito, you are 193
springs beyond the sun—and in the village
of Ixtlan, there are no Zapotecs
left to remember.
      You are on my calendar
here in California, and this morning
there is the tablecloth with the crumbs
of despair left over from every democratic thing. . . .

Thank goodness the mockingbirds are starting up,
I had almost forgotten what world
I was living in—
      I turn from my desk to their dither,
their desires and grievances boiling up
with a new regime of light,
      and I can almost
see the first golden streams of Monarchs lifting
from the conifers of Michoacan,
      their hearts
no heavier than mist releasing to the sun
as they guide back north through the industrial clouds,
past the loggers in complicity with the standard
corporations of death.
      Once, Benito, the trees pointed
the way and the stars fluttered above us like
Platonic ideals—
      I too gave assent to them
and everything larger than ourselves, but for days
I've been looking over the shoulder of dust—
which is everything that became of land reform—
and at times like these, the council of the wind
proves useless.
      If I have a soul, it's lost
inside my shirt—I always expected more
of my blood,
      which still sings of the sea,
the chorus of salt—but like the Monarchs,

we are not even the dust we leave behind.
I deliver my petitions to the waves
and receive the recapitulation of loss,
which is the old response—the shells,
the sea weed washing in with their worth.
There is no remedy in the maps of the sky;
the civic documents pile up against the poor.

I can propose anything on this bright new air,
but I won't hold my breath,
given the spindrift, the equivocations of light.
I no longer have a child's heart—
despite sea water in every cell,
the crystals of desire, the corollary
of the stars—their threads evaporating
for centuries on the surface
and representing nothing.
                                        I resign
my failed scholarship, my love
of the stars. I make my interpretations
of the lemon and eucalyptus leaves—
I hide whatever belongings I have left
from the sky.
                        President, old Governor,
compadre in dust, all the theories fail—
it's only this ordinary bird who is bothered
finally, who still carries forward our demands.
From several possibilities each morning
we will reach for hope, every time, on the branch
of hopeless things.
                                Today, in our bare feet,
this new season is everything that's sure
on earth, the earth that will never be divided
equally among any of us—
                                        at best,
and at long last, we drift through the air
no more than the dreams from trees.

Photograph of Myself—Monastery of Monte Toro Menorca elv. 1,162 ft.

for Nadya

God almighty, I'm almost half way glorious in this
gold hounds tooth coat from the local Thrift,

all my sins left behind—you can tell by the way
so much light has gathered to reflect off the crown
of my head, shining white as that angel's gown

in the high glazed sky behind me, as if I too were called
into this life, stripped of grief and God's detachment.

20 years, and I'm mildly ecstatic, on sabbatical at last,
slow as a sleepwalker down any dream bright road
that will happily have him, that will offer the dispensation
of the sun, a redemption of poppies and marguerites. . . .

Even after all the bad blood of childhood washed down
the Catholic aisles, it's fine to be here, on the sacred top

of this world, where Benedictines maintain the Blessed Mother
gave them a sign to build—the Bull of Faith in an aureate cloud
atop this table of rock. I'm just breathing the beatific air

of pines, and what interests me is the mezzanine of clouds,
the level of the sky that strains the daylight down walls

the color of clouds, and at the entrance to the parking lot,
the statue of Christ raising his arms toward heaven,
or Ibiza, and that satellite dish with its red
lightning bolt of the old gods defunct behind him,

and the burnt-out tower of the TV station
which appropriated this spot closest to the sky.

Below, tides all around this rock, and each salt parable
of the sea turning like mist toward light, the Spanish
circumstance of pain to an arduous life—the procession

of penitents, ladies with bad knees and good leather shoes,
walking the tortured curves of asphalt to the top.

I ascended by car, my life lifted a while from the world
of the faithless—I came for the view end to end
of the island, for the picnic benches under the trees,
and standing in the parking lot before the cloud-white

parapets of faith, wondered if flower-like I might turn
back a little to belief, or at least to the joy in the pale music

of the skies. In this snapshot, I could be anyone
playing it safe on Sunday—God off beyond these clouds—
indifferent enough finally that I am almost smiling,

unbothered for the first time in years. I have left
my sword and shield on the empty shore, and the truth is

I want to go no higher than the immediate deliverance
of pines and picnic tables along this ledge from where
I can see, faintly to the west, the high cliffs of Mallorca,
the business of the world held off behind a mist.

I praise the fresh bread and semi-curado cheese
with its dram of ewes milk, the tart acceptable wine

from Peñedes, the dead lunch meats we've brought along
at some sacrifice to celebrate ourselves. I praise the birds
who continue to bribe the air with song—I hold my heart

out to the wind, open collared, in my ragged coat, and
want everything, at 48, still left to me under the sky.

Watchful—Es Castell, Menorca

But the truth is that we are always
watchful, lying in wait for ourselves.

—Neruda

I remember the idiot in the town square
of Es Castell, trying each day to entice
the resident pigeons to eat the orange peels
he threw blissfully, and with hope,
on to the grass and walks.
                                        But, after so much time,
they were on to him, and the worthless peels,
and waddled away in a mumbling cloud
of feathers. . . . And each day he'd finally tire
of their truculence and unzip the jacket
of his purple warm-up suit, spread it wide
as a red kite's wings, and run
into their grey midst, scattering them
a few feet beyond the fountains, but never out
above the sky-colored water,
or into the water-colored sky. . . .

Like the old men already sitting there
in the wet shadows on the benches,
we soon tolerated him—like the pigeons
who came back in a minute or two
and who seemed to forget,
as he did, such purposeless and
momentary confrontations—days
like lost clouds.
                            I soon realized
that I was blessed simply
to walk out each morning
around the square and hear
the clock tower above the post office
strike the hour two times,
a few minutes apart, and not care
which could be correct; blessed
to sit next to the public phones,
which occasionally rang for no one,
and watch the bees dissolve into the sun,
knowing someone else had done the math of light—

the stars never showing any sign
of distress.
    Yet, if there is some great truth
about us, it's not in the stars,
or in the cluster of orange peels
almost as brilliant on the mid-morning walk—
but perhaps in the fact that we can tolerate
one among us to whom they are of equal
consequence.
    I no longer need to look
to stars, the poorly punctuated dark,
for no matter what I tap out on the Olivetti,
the earth still looks inescapable from here.
But if some innocence remains,
a little of it might be here
on this small island
deserted in winter by tourists,
foreign commerce, and even the attention
of the more fashionable birds.
The green finch and the swifts are
content and have their say.
The boats are in each afternoon,
gulls climbing the air after them,
praising the fruits of the sea.

And if now we are not sure
what is of value—looking out
at the fig trees thin as refugees
along the cliff—we at least understand
what is worthless before our eyes
morning after morning, as the steam
and fog of industry lift off
beyond the port and to the west
without us.
    I sit above the harbor,
happily on the benches provided
by the *ayuntamiento* for just this purpose,

beneath the orderly palms,
freighters and cruise ships slipping
in and out, going somewhere . . .
and make do with the intuition of wind,
the pines with their impromptu rhythms,
my hands and feet free
to defeat the intricate purposes of air,
to do nothing more than claim
the prosperity of light.
                                      Late afternoon,
I like the white tables fronting
the bars in the square, relaxing
with a small Estrella—a beer
named for a star—knowing that,
soon enough, around the corner,
I'll be on my way back
from the market and bakery
with a heart as full as the summer
5:00 sun, with a yellow grocery bag
in each hand as I ascend the steps
to our flat over the cove, where
I'll look out, and see in the reflection
of the glass doors, a happy man
arranging oranges in a bowl.

Metaphysical Trees

I still had two friends, but they were trees.

—*Larry Levis*

I went out into the woods today, and it made me feel, you know, sort of religious.

—*William Matthews*

I'd like to have a eucalyptus,
a pale and slender one bouncing its loose thoughts
off the blue—
                and maybe an avocado
with boughs like an anaconda,

and one expansive sycamore reaching out
for everything.
              Yes, and a jacaranda,
its violet shade each June edging
the eternal past . . .
                 and a pomegranate,
I want a pomegranate with Spanish flame-
red blossoms dazzling as all get-out
in dim December.
              While I'm at it,
I'll have an acacia, and a few Russian olives—
their aqua-marine leaves recalling, of course,
the implacable sea.
             And a podocarpus,
like those leaves Leonardo invented
to dovetail with the aureate cloud of light
backing up the renaissance.
              And all this
in a little valley arrived at through mustard weed
and fennel, white and lavender blooms of wild radish
recalling the loosely affiliated clouds,
the preliminary stars. . . .
            We stepped down
from that quantum shine
              clueless as to how
our bodies might be simply pronouns,
                how we stood for—
part and particle—those astral antecedents.

Right off, looking up,
                    comparing ourselves
to the lustrous night, we complained
                              of our unadorned
surroundings;
              we would have towers,
would crawl back up the stellar imbrications
despite a prohibited tree
                    and all the knowledge
we would assume,
                despite the gardens
of Nebuchadnezzar and Assurbanipal where
the dim substance of the soul was
                              elucidated
against the incomparable chastity of the sky.
And though Socrates tells us that we can learn
nothing from trees—
                only from the moral man—
what about steadfastness, fortitude, perseverance,
loyalty, tenacity, not to mention
                              modesty, grace,
their spiritual arms,
                    and a dozen other abstractions
for which men die miserably?
                        Still, we are not that bad off
if we can get out
                one afternoon and find a faithful conifer
or two to praise,
                or can let the lacy shag of a pimiento
sort out the sun,
                or especially if we can recall
the arboretum of childhood
                        and keep the camphor trees,
the pittosporum hedge in perspective
                              against the vanishing point
on the air. . . .
              But something was kept from us,

held over our heads, it seems, ever since—
                                        incantations,
the chalk and diagrams of constellations
                                    blowing by
until Latin phrases for all we were sure about
in the firmament
                        were inscribed in stone
over the cathedral doors and
                            set down darkly in orthodox
moveable type,
                    and the world divided, and so many
taking refuge for ages in the woods. . . .

Nevertheless, coming over the dark plateau,
there is our old town
                            spinning alone in light,
blister of a moon
                        against midnight, white static
of starlight across the desert, the salt coming to the surface,
the ice caps evaporating,
                            and it's November in Palm Springs,
where I go walking in the morning
                                to uncloud my heart,
to keep its tumbling, root-like
                            chemistry clear,
to see four wild parrots fly from palm to palm as I pass
the convention center,
                        the steamy perfume of stalks and delphiniums
rising from the moist beds . . .
                        and I am 7 or 8 again
wearing a red bow tie and stiff blue
                            business suit for Easter,
the glory of the manifest world
                        arranged in sunlight.
                Above me, the mimosa and lemon boughs,
and no text beyond that—
                        I mean we're protected

from the vast void of space
                              by nothing more than air,
and when the night calms
                              down to darkness
                                             we listen
for the planets whirling by
                              and it's only the trees
giving us back our breath. . . .

I take those wild parrots, brilliant and green as Eden,
as a sign from God,
                      admittedly a God largely uninterested,
unsure perhaps
                of what more we could possibly want—
magnolia, banyan, yew?
                         Maybe an indifferent sign,
indecipherable, inadvertent,
                              but there are at least these
four green clues to some happiness beneath the sky. . . .

If I can't have trees, then perhaps someday
just a few yards of dirt,
                           some fennel bushes and nasturtiums—
that portion of childhood
                           still volunteering from the roadside,
beckoning in the winds of traffic.
                                   For the time being
I'll take these parrots appropriating
                                 the tops of the royal palms
as if everything were still ours
                              equally before the sun.
Take what you can,
                    you know what God will do—
he will let the complaints rise
                              like a little smoke

dissolving against the dawn;
                          he will turn away,
                                        thinking perhaps
of another universe.
                    The oceans will warm
                              and drive the sail fish north,
the last log will be rolled out of the Amazon—
                             it will all go
to hell
        in a corporate hand basket as we're tipping
the brim of our hat
                  over our eyes, nodding-out on the bench
in the blue
            absolution of shade,
                       beneath the last trees
of our forgiveness.

To Ernesto Trejo in the Other World

Still tonight, the stars are where we left them,
nonchalant, incontestable in their distance.

Once we were those stars—all of us atoms
no memory will admit. And once it mattered

what we made of stars, and read into the sky;
but now all the theories scatter like blackbirds

from a field, there, against the unrequited blue.
I have no idea, truly, where you are—dry wind

in eucalyptus, sedan of clouds pearl-edged in the west.
The soul could well be that cloud in the empty shape

of clouds given the spare charities of Time, the breeze
that sweeps any of us away. I wonder if you see

the winos who never left The Eagle Café, the solar systems
of grease spinning on the blue plate specials, if you can

see Spain, a country you never knew? Speculation is
you overlook it all, can look down Diagonal or out 46,

stone-blazing afternoons in Madera or Madrid, or in
Barcelona, the evening walking bejeweled into the bay.

In Fresno, I remember only one guitar that spoke
of the sea, and a cypress or two along Van Ness,

and no sea of course, no Ramblas with caged birds
reciting in their paradisiacal tongues, no dusty angels

high in the sycamores who, if they could, would descend
for a drink at one of the chrome tables in the shade.

So many gone now, who knows if you could meet anyone
on Olive Street and praise the poets of Spain?

We never spoke of the Alhambra, the refrain of waves
at Castelldefels, the lost continents of the moon.

Whatever is out there is here, just as well. And so
I think of Rome where Giordano Bruno proclaimed

a plurality of worlds, a belief I almost maintain,
excepting the examinations by iron and fire.

And so crows today are just crows, happy to hop about
suburban lawns without an inner life. This is the world

and it all happens here—nothing else stands for the sky,
weak and frayed as it is with our conjecture. Nevertheless,

I accede to the a lyric mantilla of stars, a mythopoeic light
filtering down far stanzas of the dark as evidence,

perhaps, of hope. There is no other light, and we have
gone through eons worth of it with less and less to show.

Is there any way, my friend, to tell us where we are
headed tonight? I cannot see beyond Miramar Point,

that small shore of childhood where I was content
with the omnipotent salt air, with the mocking bird

impromptu in the pines, where I stand, feet in the cold
sand, a tide rising, the sea reflecting the clear light

of space back into space—the anaphora of the heart
holding on before God, or light, or none of the above.

Old News: Poem on a Birthday

> Whatsoever of it has flown away is past;
> Whatsoever of it remains is future.
>
> —*St. Augustine, Confessions, XI*

When it came down to it, I loved the '50s, the spectacular black
      and white winter nights, starlight dusting down

shiny and crystalline as Phenobarbital, a fleet of drowsy angels
      drifting over the car lots and department stores

as I waited in the front seat of the old Pontiac for my father
      to come out of the radio station, the call letters

over the door humming their pink neon like a distant nebula.
      Now at 55, grey matter drying up like the river-

bank clay it really is, I can still recognize a young Sinatra,
      on "Street of Dreams," and see the white hot dog

wrappers fluttering along the foul line at Ebbets Field on TV,
      and the grey phrasing of that soft, lost light.

I was sure then that the slow progress of days was in my debt,
      that I was due some great fate or adulation

for just breathing in style among my friends, for we started out
      thinking we knew all that was hidden in the air—

where, perhaps, we were finally headed with our half dollar
      souls, like the star beam burning homeward

in the bird's breast, the salt glaze rising off the froth of waves
      in our image—less and less always in our arms.

*

These days, all of my friends are going to Italy—soon, every bit
      of the past we know will pass us by. Beneath

the umbrella pines, along the scored basalt road into the ruins,
      there are things I remember remembering there

surely from another life—same air, same thick sun, familiar
  dust settling in the mind come evening, or

on the road through the Etruscan hill town, some deep
  blue tiles surrounding the fountain

one afternoon like pieces of the Aegean winking back?
  Either way, it's nice being here, sky thinning,

a cloud tipped over the sea like one of God's discarded
  helmets. Once I would have asked for help,

for the intercession of the winds to carry me off beyond
  the broken ankle of light at Point Conception,

but today it's enough to be next to nowhere in California,
  though in the photo on my desk I sit

with my grandfather on a crate in an orange grove
  in Florida, in 1950, the world looking fine

as far as I can see. I'm wearing shorts and a baseball cap,
  staring off into the horizon as if he were

always going to be there and not just in the speechless light
  of a photograph, and not just in the approaching

dark 50 years later—the grainy finish not picking up my
  tiny wings which will leave me, mid-air,

before I'm seven. But that's me all the same, an orange
  in my hands, right leg shorter than the left—

sun generous in winter there, a white sky, and who knew
  what mattered as I was stupefied, too close

to the invisible impasse above me to interpret a time
      when everything was all already ours . . .

the dark flame-shaped leaves, daylight dividing the rows,
      rehearsing its comings and goings among

the living, while I breathed the blue air and the sky looked
      right through us as if it were nothing,

or we little more than that for wondering how we could
      ever be the stardust at the start of things.

Poem after Lu Yu

I've been reading the Chinese again, and
              there is still everything
                        to steal from—

the entire world, whenever you have time
              to put down your bundle of sticks . . .
                        a hundred themes like

thin clouds drifting by, christened by the moon . . .
              Boughs of the mimosas move
                        with all the improbable

weight of the invisible, but I have my thoughts,
              and space is endless. The empty
                        wine bottles squint

with starlight, the usual troubles evaporate.
              The business of heaven blows by
                        out there, and from this

vantage point, is the business of heaven,
              out there . . . And so my company is
                        again a few despondent

clouds—unlike water though, the days sail off
              and do not circle back—such
                        pity for the years

which come and go in the open window
              with a light breeze, with the ancient
                        poet's lines recalling

his boyhood in Yen Chao, a river at Tsa-feng.
              Hundreds of years and half the world
                        between us, but what are

the differences now? Already I am lonely
              with the old dust and bitterness
                        of the Milky Way.

Philosophical Poem on the Usual Subjects

> I don't need to write memos and letters every
> morning. Others will take over, always with
> the same hope, the one we know is senseless
> and devote our lives to.
>
> —*Milosz*

The stars come slowly out as if someone were calling them
        by name into the sky—surely

We are as essential as the stars? And as lonely. And for their part
        the trees contribute nothing new—

Though on any given night they seem to read our thoughts
        before the apparently empty sky.

Nonetheless, there's often something singing above us—
        dry wind in the olive leaves, only

September and three fires already in the chaparral; wind
        chorusing in the flames as well, ash

Floating out to sea and back again, like guilt, like pride.
        I understand that, having taught

Greek tragedy M & W at 3:00—the burnished stanzas
        of suffering glimmering briefly

Like October leaves—God, Fate, what-have-you—an allegory
        with which to face those stars.

For good measure, I sometimes mix in a theory about the collapse
        of the universe. Some thin clouds

Cast shadows over the geraniums—a suggestion of an afterlife,
        compelling as any. What have I been

Up to all these years, searching for a trap door in the blue,
        the soul I left disguised among

The shining trees of childhood, in the foam off ocean waves—
       every road you can never take again?

*

My blood knows the insinuations of salt, a sea tugging at my
       shirt sleeve. I could retire

In the elements, dispassionate as air, little more than the salt-
       colored clouds lifted back to sea—

Our interpretations of events having passed through our porous brains,
       turning us like flowers for the light

When we are done worrying about our molecules colliding and
       starlight ending it all in the cold

Conundrum of space. Above the clouds, all the resolutions
       are walking without shoes.

*

The clouds of the 20th century are gone—so much for my inheritance.
       Make what you will of them, where else

Do we resemble the infinite? Fog is the likely interpretation of the past.
       I'm left with the white collar

Around the hills—and the hills broken down like old shoes at the edges—
       such dog loneliness as there is

Beneath the yellow camphor boughs. You're over 50, you're going
       to die. With so much sand in those shoes

Who can remember back to the angels we first were? No fish-tailing
       now in that old Chevrolet, the bent wings

Of its tail fins cutting across the back road home and bouncing you,
       without a bruise, off the sycamores.

No point now in being clever? What shall we compare life to today?
    The old coat, the shoe, the onion as emblem

Of the soul? The trees have nothing but themselves; a net of sunlight
    drags the bottom of a pool and I suppose

It should not matter that nothing rises to the surface. So it is
    with Desire, the considered imagery

Of our lives. So it is with Hope, that small bird sleeping in my chest,
    its obscure, incontestable song.

Memory

> The fish's soul
>> is his empty bones.
>
>> —*Yehuda Amichai*

We would lie then along the cloud-grey sand,
      in our cool unconscious youth,
in the overhanging bruises of the eucalyptus, our eyes
      filling with the watery apparatus
of the abstract and washed-out blue, day-dreaming
      through the daffodil light of Judy Holliday
in "Bells Are Ringing" or Sandra Dee in "A Summer Place."
      We didn't have the first idea about ideas,
and, diving beneath kelp beds, shot the carefree fish
      with our hand-sling spears and never gave
a thought to what the trident symbolized—a soul
      was only something in a catechism text,
an emptiness in the air we were never going to touch,
      unlike the Eucharist-white bones of the fish.
And when the only bass I ever speared wriggled
      on the tines in the bright and awful air,
the slash in its side unfolded like bread soaked in wine,
      and its amber eye beheld me there and all the sky
could see who I was and had become with its ichor
      oozing on my sea-stained hands. And still
what sweet vowels the plovers and godwits sent up
      despite me in my frogman flippers and mask
that disguised so little as I thrust my stick and defied
      next to nothing in the sky. The gulls praised
the body of the world, and flew their grey rags of death,
      and loitered on the logs and seaweed there—
patient again as death—to see what I would do. And though
      wave after wave testified against me, I knew
no sorrow, and felt innocent as sea foam, unassailed
      as the blue-roofed bungalows of the resort,
the weekenders on the boardwalk, the ice plant
      over the seawall and the dunes. Everything
was, for the most part, unknown—the ridicule in the wind,
      the resurrection of dust, my spindrift breath,
and the ocean's churning roots—just driftwood bumping,
      beached forever—the sea wrack of the heart.

Wooden Boats

Tierra del Fuego, Punta Arenas, Magellan,
Vasco de Gama, Juan Rodriquez Cabrillo,
or Gaspar de Portola—1958
and I had all the answers
in Miss Vasquez's Geography Class.
I knew the New World as it was known,
as they declaimed it 400 years ago,
from their decks in San Diego, San Francisco,
the Bay of Monterey,
                    thinking
they knew all there was to know. . . .
But every 50 years a wind comes up
from nowhere, facts scuttle
like dry leaves on a pond,
and the universe changes again,
as, empty-headed before the sky,
we look down to our worthless notes
beneath the desk.
                    Now the invisible,
once impossible, sub-atomic particles
spin in theoretical defiance
of most every rule Einstein
put in the book.
                    And those tired souls
dragging back from work on the #26 bus,
the few silhouettes briefly before
the sea-green windows, they are all
we will likely know of illumination.
A heavy marine layer arrives each spring,
a full moon, dull as a trash can lid,
a lapsed atmosphere where we are
perhaps finally headed with our non-
essential salts and dust.
                    Romantics
still believe there is time to reaffix
the blue, to redefine the space
where we might find ourselves

reflected in the first bright dimension
of our dreams.
                    So much has been
taken away while somewhere in the universe
no time has gone by at all. . . .
We recheck our charts about
the provinces and protectorates
of the past, the stalled longitude
of hope, and are left with nothing
that will help us homeward—
though we walk out each dawn
with the white clouds becalmed,
having claimed it all.

Loyalty

My father knew next to nothing, really,
        about how to live this life—
business partners stole him blind;
        he had no friends and never
drank. Even Jean Paul Sartre could get
        sentimental after three martinis
and some saxophone music, but my father
        was serious about advertising,
knew the fix was in on the network news,
        all the professors were communist
dupes. But he maintained a clear affection
        for the abstract theme of stars,
always taking a minute to point overhead
        to the beamy sky in Montecito,
long before the '60s and all our industrial
        radiance and silt clouded our clear
view outward. He'd talk about space—flying
        saucers, life on other worlds, time
disappearing at the speed of light, whirligigs
        and flywheels of the cosmos that
assumed significance for him, an intangible
        but bona fide machinery reflecting us. . . .
He pledged allegiance to the vast unknown—
        yet another thing he was somehow
smugly sure he was certain of. I had been
        drilled by the forbidding priests
and nuns, and one take on the dim and indefinite
        to me seemed as valid as the next.
But he discerned no conspiracy in the stars,
        no secret in the silvered edge
of air that would not save us from the burden
        of the dark. I was seven, or eight,
and on the swings each day at school flew
        upside down in the blue cup
of the world, and it was all the same to me
        as I pulled the sky through my lungs

and scanned the enjambed grey line of clouds
        for any lost music, any foundation
for the casual delight that must have been
        taken in the seas set spinning,
in the collective fidelity of our hearts, here
        in the middle distance from the sun.

The trees of my childhood shook their heads
        as I outdistanced myself with
speculation—alone with the wind's thin strings,
        believing I saw the light
of our souls floating on the coattails
        of a storm, or in the white caps'
salt dust. And mornings now I catch myself
        complaining with the finches
in a buddleia bush, with the brigade of starlings
        who have something persistent
to say about who will inherit the earth.
        Again today, I want to write something
without clouds in it, without loss, without whatever
        it was that the wind blew through
without a trace, engaged as I am in devotion,
        in subterfuge on my own behalf.
My father who was burned back to star dust
        and scattered over the sea.

The Uncertainty Principle

The stars above us actually aren't . . .
they're just pin-balled
every which way, pitching about
in the galactic swill—scads of them
like pebbles the ocean drags back
in its moon-tide and ebb.
                              Our atoms
no different, derived from theirs,
shining until we likewise are
decompressed with time
and float out to darkness.
                              At least
we think it's time we're looking at
out there as we add our short run up
and develop our takes on nebulae
still popping like '50s flash bulbs,
paparazzi of death at the far end
of any lens, despite whatever zoom out
to deep distance or wide-angle,
the fish-eye of the infinite.
                              Quasars,
missing matter, black holes—variables
of a cosmic throw of the dice—amino acids,
salt water and a comet's hodgepodge of filched
chemicals that have consciousness
rising like steam off a primordial soup.
Who can do the math, the likelihood
of mammals advancing upright
over the grassy planes ?
                              The past
contains everything—red-shifted
like a freight train speeding off
into Kansas, bringing the near and far
loss of childhood home each night,
and each of us equally impoverished in that.
Yet everything else is still
going to happen somewhere—so what
are we to believe?

How then
does Heisenberg's Principle—
the mechanical quantum sophistry—
help us? By his own admission,
it's impossible to determine
the speed and location
of an object because energy
and momentum are exchanged
just looking, and this spoils
the original details of the system.
The laws of cause and effect then
don't apply, but in 1932
they gave him the Nobel anyway.
Perhaps the reductive analogy helps:
whatever is observed is changed
by the observation. How then
will our true natures, let alone
the light-clogged patterns
of other galaxies—ever be known,
if God—as Sister Caritas proclaimed
on the first day of school—is in fact
watching us?
        So here I am,
evening coming in, the sky
staggering off through the trees,
and I feel as artless as the air,
my mind's unsteady thoughts
blowing around, straw in a breeze. . . .
I have no idea how far
these few clouds will get
across the sky; I've rounded them off
to the nearest zero,
but have lost count on the high
blackboard of the blue—
most likely I should ask nothing
of anything beyond the air,
given how much evidence
has escaped us.

           Each day
the clouds enter a new world,
never what they were, every
anecdote and historical bit
of us they've overlooked, scattered
like flash-cards and left
behind them.
               You offer one reason
or another—the earth is made
of fire, or air, or water, rarefied
and condensed—of leptons, muons,
or quarks, left handed, right handed
or charmed, and what reason
has the sky to listen?
               Nobody
asked you. Each evening brings
to mind all the still space where
we are not—and even with the first
underestimated equation of the seas
to fall back on, the formulas
for splendor seem to be random,
unaccounted for, and few.

Photograph of John Berryman on the Back of *Love & Fame*

I have no idea whether we live again.

—*John Berryman*

I see the man who wrote his 11 intemperate letters
to the Lord is the man half grateful near his end,
a man almost at ease and deep behind his whiskers here.
A charmer who won't be completely run to ground,

grizzled as the granite going to pieces at his back,
he's channeling his last cloud-split reasoning
directly at the doubtful sky, uncovering any worth
or last ditch redeeming chance, and carefully

subscribing to that. Who then knows about the soul—
chipped away with age, grey with cosmic grit,
some evanescent paste holding together beyond
our bones? I have some interest in this late line

of questioning, that desperate dodge and grab at
conviction while balancing on one foot, the sinking
weight of everything you likely know on the other.
I have a friend who revered and loved the man, as,

I imagine, God intended us to respect that knot
of light burning in the rare and fervent few among us.
33 years ago, Berryman posed, nonchalant
before the lens in Ireland—Latinate, distilled,

high lonesome and jazzy riffs mixed with reflex
and a syntactic ear for idiosyncrasy, inward
somnambulism—a sober self-estimate that held him
steady amid the wobbling flames, dreaming

in the distracted atmosphere with love and fame
trailing a ways off from where he later waved
then stepped away, dawdling toward the glory
of the dust. For a man who could not much love

himself he came generous with his love and trust
at last in God. O, time wears us away to little
more than salt or sea air—here or elsewhere, but how
to know which metaphysical hammerlock's going

to pin us down the years and force capitulation?
Yet, he's still credible, walking the edge, a famous
sparkle of doubt in the eyes, teetering in the blind
up-drafts of belief—both sides of the street in play,

sand beneath the soft soles of his feet. He expects
to fall and will blame, ex post facto and no doubt
rightly, logically so, God, when he is not there,
to swoosh out of the unphysical aether to hold,

metaphorically, his hand, in His infinite one,
that ardent strophe of flesh and blood above
the common traffic of the world, where sooner or
later all our blood and bony minds fall to wreck

one afternoon. One day to the next, I find myself
as reasonably sure as Berryman about the afterlife,
and I would, at 50-something, line up behind him,
my right hand raised into the air in hope of one.

But my heart's not finally in it; it's still half bitter
like a root vegetable they always said was good
for you, and so will not likely lift me, heavy out
of this world, as his must have—singing, praising

purely the fog-thick invisible source, the blind-
spot in creation sustained by desperate lines,
and he dead-grateful for his gift, disavowing
eloquence alone. Yet somehow he firmly clutched

in one mildly shaking hand a glass half-full of Faith.
For any proof, I have only, as I said, the friend who
knew him, this photo, his clipped and thorny song—
the conflicted pledges of an absent minded God. . . .

Travel

I have never been to Buenos Aires, or Juan-les-Pins
        for that matter, except in the dark

'40s and '50s films—and it was never Jean Seberg or
        Ingrid Bergman who ran up to me, shaking

the gold ocean from her short hair, looking into my eyes
        with all the lost minutes a black & white sea

withheld. Yet I recall the tangerine suns and sapphire
        lagoons on postcards of French Polynesia,

awash in junk shop drawers, and a lavish night sky
        over Yosemite, that deep blue table cloth

and the bread-crumb stars spinning evenly away from us
        toward a barricade of bright islands

we are never going to see. In this way, we received
        more darkness than light—the 10 percent

that escaped on the blast at the start, our souvenir
        of somewhere we've never been. Dreamers,

walkers in our easy sleep, we unfolded our arms and
        filled them with the lost destinations,

the local outskirts of the air, with the last image of the sea
        which compares us to clouds under sail,

in transit to who knows where. Sundown, and the shore
        birds head homeward with the song

that first pulled them away—the sky, like everything,
        still unresolved. You can hear the dark

rustling overhead, the sky we can never return to, empty-
    handed as we are with only our obvious

hearts as guide. Any way you look at it, it's a long way
    to go to have only come this far.

2007–2014

Poverty

for Phil

la colera de pobre
tiene dos rios contra muchos mares.

— *Cesar Vallejo*

Vallejo wrote that with God we are all orphans.
I send $22 a month to a kid in Ecuador
so starvation keeps moving on its bony burro
past his door—no cars, computers,
basketball shoes—not a bottle cap
of hope for the life ahead . . . just enough
to keep hunger shuffling by in a low cloud
of flies. It's the least I can do,
and so I do it.
           I have followed the dry length
of Mission Creek to the sea and forgotten to pray
for the creosote, the blue salvia, let alone
for pork bellies, soy bean futures.
                      Listen.
There are 900 thousand Avon Ladies in Brazil.
Billions are spent each year on beauty products
world-wide—28 billion on hair care, 14 on skin
conditioners, despite children digging on the dumps,
selling their kidneys, anything that is briefly theirs.
9 billion a month for war in Iraq, a chicken bone
for foreign aid.
           I am the prince of small potatoes,
I deny them nothing who come to me beseeching
the crusts I have to give. I have no grounds for complaint,
though deep down, where it's anyone's guess,
I covet everything that goes along with the illustrious—
creased pants as I stroll down the glittering boulevard,
a little aperitif beneath Italian pines. But who cares
what I wear, or drink? The rain? No, the rain is something
we share—it devours the beginning and the end.

The old stars tumble out of their bleak rooms like dice—
Box Cars, Snake Eyes, And-The-Horse-You-Rode-In-On . . .
not one metaphorical bread crumb in tow.
Not a single *Saludo!* from the patronizers

of the working class—Pharaoh Oil, Congress,
or The Commissioner of Baseball—all who will eventually
take the same trolley car to hell, or a slag heap
on the outskirts of Cleveland.
                          I have an ATM card,
AAA *Plus* card. I can get cash from machines, be towed
20 miles to a service station. Where do I get off penciling in
disillusionment? My bones are as worthless as the next guy's
against the stars, against the time it takes light to expend
its currency across the cosmic vault. I have what everyone has—
the over-drawn statement of the air, my blood newly rich
with oxygen before the inescapable proscenium of the dark,
my breath going out equally with any atom of weariness
or joy, each one of which is closer to God than I.

We Need Philosophers for This?

for Gary DeVito, 1947–2007

I'd like to grab Nietzsche by the collar
of his long coat, slap the cigar from his mouth
and say, "OK wise guy, where do all the big ideas,
get us?" I can't close my eyes for a split second
and not see poor DeVito's face, the chiseled
spitting image of movie star Gilbert Roland,
that face that got him out of a hundred jams,
that had him thinking he could get away
with anything until his draft notice came.

I want Nietzsche to study Gary's happy brain
running loose as rain water in the highlands
north of Pleiku, Gary living in a loin cloth
with the Montagnards, smoking that resin-
soaked weed, beyond good and evil, believing
half of everything Nietzsche wrote without
ever having read a word.
                                    Gary who was
mildly existential without ever speaking
a sentence in French, who was never going
to fall in line with the press and polish
of orthodox materialism, who was taken back
at gun point by force-recon guys who,
dark as ghosts, humped it umpteen klicks
up river to haul him out without his pipe
and the Chief's daughter whom he'd married
without a second thought, who were
ordered to be sure that every last grunt
was squared-away.
                                    Gary heard the music
of Nietzsche's friend Wagner one time only,
in Coppola's film blasting from the helicopters
swooping down like Valkyries on the VC,
the way it never happened. And he wasn't
coming back to the world by a long shot,
even after 30 years in the Post Office
and 5 DUIs.

Schopenhauer was right
about the eternal torment of desire,
and he didn't surf. Tug on Spinoza's
shirt sleeve as we might, he'd never
come up with anything in Jesus' name to save
Gary from his last trouble, forgetting
he was 60 and still chasing skirt into Motel 6,
a little chemical boost for the blood
despite all the tipsy electricity of the heart
about to short out and shut down—
zap, *muy pronto*—bad luck, free radicals,
karma, or recessive genes, pick one.

Ralph Waldo Emerson would have
told him to stay put in the jungle as long
as someone was bringing in lunch and
the correspondence. What good would it do
to listen again to the Padre Choristers
in the Old Mission's Christmas Midnight Mass
except that he might hear the distant harmony
of leaves in the crowns of bamboo,
and the temple bells?
                        He should have realized
he was no superman, that his rational faculties
could collapse in Carpinteria as easily as in Turin,
in the Piazza Carlo Alberto, where Nietzsche's grip
on the nature of being slipped away one afternoon
as he threw his arms around the neck of a horse
being whipped, looked into its eyes, and asked,
My God, why are we so unhappy?

I Too Am Not a Keeper of Sheep: Variation on a Theme by Pessoa

> There's metaphysics enough in not thinking about anything.
> —*Fernando Pessoa*

What's following me around these days, I don't know—at least
    it isn't self pity, a bum with a bitter cup of coffee
        from the convenience store mumbling

next to me on the bench. For each evening I'm comforted,
    sitting here, thinking backwards, watching as those
        gauzy abstractions of my youth

with their berets and French unfiltered cigarettes and dogma
    are devoured like Pharaoh's army by the great grey
        jawbones of the sea as the fog advances.

And it's not the miasma of middle age, not unless I'm going
    to live to 116. Done with that, I still take a great delight
        in breaking off a bright armful of gladioli

from the abandoned beds by the library—a little defiance
    to everything.... For meaning, I drift back
        as far as the reeds and river bed,

thumb through my old Geography text to what we called
    Asia Minor, where it could just as easily have been
        my atoms as Aristotle's, suspended

in the dust above an Aegean port, glimmering like anything
    for sale. How I wandered through the aethers
        to arrive here can only be explained

by the chaotic logic of matter as it reorganizes itself, the spin
    a little light puts on it all. However, thinking alone
        has, it seems, never accounted for much

happiness. Why, if there is a God overlooking the shrubs,
    should He be concerned with me, obstinate and
        agnostic as I've grown ever since

the Dodgers left Brooklyn, and that idiot Timmy Armour
tossed my Wilson Bob Feller mitt by the classroom
door for any unconscionable kid

to steal, and who, 46 years and counting, has yet to apologize or
make restitution, if such could possibly be made
for that supple sun yellow steer hide

glove that snagged the visible and invisible whistling by
my ear at Third. It was the singular illumination
of my sullen youth, the only unyielding

source beyond the truthless, confabulated tales of parochial school.
If I have a soul, there is only a string now holding it
down as I float here on the cliff

above the Pacific, like the lantana or sea vetch at the mercy
of any change in wind. So how, in their insolence
and apostasy, could I not admire

the industrial brotherhood of crows over my shoulder, their fearlessness
before the blue, as they sit in the coral tree,
blossoms flaming all around them,

redeemed in their own darkness? If we do come back, I wouldn't
want to be one of them—every day just a day
away from starving, trying

to pick the pocket of circumstance, never sure of the next crust.
Nothing's worth giving up knowing that I don't
know, the plain improbability of Life

Ever After, as we were made to pray every day. Oxygen,
for instance, is an implicit theology—the proof
is in continuing to breathe,

in any tree drawing up water wordlessly, answering its own
        prayer. Whatever thoughts I have, I'm happy
                to let them wander away like clouds,

beyond explanation—like a few sheep grazing aimlessly
        downhill toward the sea, where there is still more
                than enough mystery to go around.

Ode to Clouds

Gauzy membranes, the ocean's stippled exhalation,
        impasto of high hats, roundabouts,
stacks of silver dollars, ampersands connecting
        ellipses that scatter the tenuous threads
of longing, attenuation of some infinite afterthought. . . .
        Oh, the impromptu sails I followed out
of ignorance, out the blue, wide windows of my school.
        Intaglio of secrets, strategies released
behind our backs and not one thing as obvious as our salt
        deeply inaccessible inside us, blood-shifted
toward the primordial—glassy bubbles working their way
        up to the gold-chained surface of the sea,
rounded up, reduced to a stamp, a brain smudge, a paring
        of snow, some crisscross of weather,
footnote to distance, to an intuitive, untranslatable
        conspiracy, not that far, it's been argued,
removed from where I still sit below, smoking
        my Nicaraguan double corona, imperator
of my garden and the western sky. Angels—I always took
        their side—ivory blossoms uncurling on
the hydroponic blue, ghosted birds of paradise, horse feathers,
        blueprint and palimpsest, it's the same sky—
Lompoc or Peloponnesus—skein of the absent mind, river bank
        and orchard of almond flowers as far as you can see.
My blood pressure goes down with white geraniums, valerian,
        and Martha Washingtons, plum leaves and
lemon verbena, pieces of their shadows drifting across the lawn,
        apostrophes to the empty afternoon.
They ride in from nowhere and are waved away like smoke.
        They approach on the idling engine of wind,
reefs and winged striations, elliptical floats, barges on a south-
        easterly flow that have the patio sun shades
lifting as if filled with life up toward the coruscated bodies
        covered with the careless fingerprints of God.
The cold salt molecules count us out from the sea, as oxygen
        links atom to atom through the translucent

text and neuroscience of air—thin as old bromides about what
        we're up to here below, where we're heading, and
what for? One or two ideas hovering that the blue jays dismiss
        in a torrent of complaint, along with beauty
and all other remarkable but tangential jottings
        referencing a mind external to it all, beginning
with my mother pinning the bed sheets up, 54 years ago
        in our backyard, Springfield, Missouri.

There I am in my paste-white toddler's shoes, wobbling
        along, the huge sheets blowing all about me
on the clothesline overhead, losing hold of childhood
        like a floss of milkweed—or there, in the back
of the Bel Air, before the dance, billows of fire
        from a pint of Four Roses and a Burgermeister
in a crumpled bag taking us up, the horizon steadily
        stretching away, a bank of pearlized altocumulus,
wind-glazed tendons of dream . . . all gone, and still up
        there somewhere—interminable reconfigurations,
spots of breath on the wind wing, the rolling of a few bones
        in the undercroft of night, the milk of wishes
spilled out like the inundation of stars when we arrived.

In Memory of the Winos at the Moreton Bay Fig Tree, Santa Barbara, CA

God knows, if God ever cared, how they managed
to scrape up the buck twenty-nine + tax most days
to buy their fifths of Night Train, Thunderbird,
Italian Swiss Colony Tokay, but they gathered
in the same small circle when they did, dull shadows
in the dull shade of the enormous limbs of the tree
at the corner of Chapala and Montecito Streets,
a stone's throw from the Southern Pacific.
                                        The tree
arrived from Australia in 1876, a sailor presenting
a seedling to a girl, and it grew to be the largest in the U.S.,
its grey and green architecture providing a makeshift chapel
of air, the knee-high buttressing roots crevices for the lost
to bunk-up by night.
                        We were kids with crew cuts
and 10-speed Schwinns, and rode from woodsy suburbs
into town when there were still four lights stopping traffic
dead in the middle of the 101. We crossed the freeway
all through the late '50s and '60s, heading up from
Cabrillo Boulevard along the beach and couldn't help
but see them, men whose hands and faces the sun had turned
the color and texture of bark. There were no "homeless" then,
only hoboes, tramps, and bums, our parents admonishing us
to avoid the tree along with the lower precincts of State Street
with its shine parlors, pool halls, and flea-bag hotels.
One day after school, Orsua and I, checking out car parts,
window-shopping by the army surplus store, were pan-handled
by a man who looked as if he'd been sleeping under a truck.
Orsua took 67¢ from his pocket and dropped it
into his grease-dark hand saying, "You have to promise me now
not to waste this on food, and go out and buy some real rot-gut."
The guy looked mystified, and we walked away laughing
like the mean, carefree kids we were long before our own futures
would pull over to the side of the curb.
                                    How could I know that
8 more years of college and graduate school and I'd wash up
on Milpas Street, working at Hi-Time Liquor, accepting handfuls

of grimy coins for white port, Wild Irish Rose, and even Manischewitz
as early as 10 a.m.? How could I know that they'd narrow State Street
to two lanes, widen the sidewalks, and chain-off the wide base of that tree
to make the lawn empty and safe from them, and so better attract
tourists and promote trade for the Junior Chamber of Commerce
who were lunching and throwing back big well-drinks at Joes,
just above where they'd cleared out the Rescue Mission
and Santa Barbara Billiards, where they'd run Casa Blanca,
the oldest Mexican restaurant in town, out of business
in favor of projectile, tree-shaking rock n roll bars shoulder
to shoulder down to the tracks?
                              Later, in my senior year,
cruising in a buddy's old Studebaker truck, we rode by
the train station where no one had arrived since 1958,
and instead of seeing the dozen or so dispossessed lying among
the thick roots—their slumped shapes hard to differentiate
from the dried piles of leaves—we saw them assemble
as one returned from across the freeway with a bottle
in a brown paper bag. We expected him to swill most of it
straight down, but, thinking of the others—abandoned
as they were by circumstance, by the roll of God's miserable dice—
he didn't.
          Gently peeling back the bag from the sea-
green throat, he unscrewed the cap, lifted his head
sunward and reverently sipped, slowly swallowing
the burning light, and was thus illuminated before
recapping the mouth, folding back the bag and passing it
to his neighbor, so that peace would settle over them,
as they did all they could to save their lives.

What Einstein Means to Me

I don't give a good goddamn
anymore what anyone thinks.
I like Albert Einstein sticking
his tongue out at the press,
J. Edgar Hoover, and everyone else
poking their nose in, in his infamous photo—
how it lightens my reckless and irregular heart
each time I see it.
         Not that I'm
offering any comparisons here,
having received my diploma
in Theoretical Physics from a home
correspondence course requiring
50 years of star-gazing and 500 box tops
of Nabisco Shredded Wheat.
I just admire the self confidence
that says, I'm a free and irresponsible agent
for my immeasurable will: There's nothing
left for them to do to me now?
         And I love
that image of him riding his bicycle
around Princeton in his 60s
without socks, legs splayed to either side
to better glide on the slapdash air,
and his electric white hair shocking the wind,
whose bare-backed imagination
had articulated the invisible
bones in most every particle known
and unknown , who went, over time,
2 out of 3 falls with God, regardless
of the outcome. . . .
         Spit into the wind,
we all know the speed of light, and that
soon enough gravity waves will slip
beneath each one of our doors.
         Back
in the day, it took a shining church key

to open a can of beer and I believe
in the simple physics that says
it would comfort more hearts and minds
to hand your fellow man a cold one
than to direct him to mind-numbing chorus
of "in excelsis deo," a warehouse of hosannas.
No matter what stellar exposition
you subscribe to, you'll still find yourself
living in 4 dimensions, unless you see time-
space as one more component of
a ride on a battered light beam,
the unreconstructed bits of a unified field
against which all the odds are stacked,
regardless of who is rolling the dice. . . .

Scattering My Mother's Ashes: Santa Barbara, CA

for Dortha Suze Miller, 1924–2008

City of my green sea days and dreams,
I wondered about everything, suspended
before me invisibly beneath the sky,
in back of the pearl-colored breakers,
the blue cliffs of air....
                         White bougainvilleas
of cloud unknotted above the palms
where I awaited the wind's consolation
like any child in the immeasurable splendor
of the sun.
               My mother's hand guided me
along the tide line and through the sleepy parks,
and we watched the gulls ascend as if
there were few mysteries on earth,
as I day-dreamed my long hours
in the grass and sweet alyssum....

Back along the shore I left
all that time ago—for reasons
that have long escaped into a melancholy
spindrift glaze—I find the fusion
of my blood and salt to be just
another bit of trace evidence that
God let slip, aside from the unusable
data about matter and light....

Everything else, he kept to himself
with the subtext of wind,
with all the unmarked files of dust.
She is gone who I thought would stand
forever between me and the stars....

Theory of Life on Other Worlds: Contemplating Retirement & Social Security Reform at Shore Line Park

Now, the mild despairs of autumn, and the wind
      shrugging its shoulders among the leaves
            have me as uncertain as ever—

all those lights discarded across the dark, over-worked . . .
      I'm just sitting here in my frayed overcoat
            of hope, out of range of philosophy

and dialectics, yet a thin music can still be extracted
      from a breeze, that same one we felt when
            we were happy beside the palms

and there seemed no great injustice at work above us
      in the stars. Now, if angels alighted out of the blue,
            I'd want to know why

they've taken their sweet time—were they delayed
      with some metaphysical/industrial action,
            and what, if anything,

do they propose to do about the past? That one with
      a Dodger cap on back-to-front, skate-boarding
            the cliff walk, looping on an edge

of wind, he'd be mocking us, right, flying by without wings?
      And the one lighting a Marlboro, his face licked
            with flame like a Mexican icon—

what's that signify, beyond everything holding on briefly
      before the dark? There are no trickle-down
            arguments for transcendence, and

in their glowing bones, it's not material to them. They could
      care less how many years I've been on the job,
            wearing these serviceable brown shoes

with heavy soles, my Chairman Mao cap missing its red star.
   Industrial/Cultural revolution, it's all old hat,
     so far as they are concerned,

and they aren't. These days, I vote for just breathing
   evenly, for the social contract and the continuing
     resolution with the trees, my membership

card in United Anarchists—if they ever issued one—
   having expired. Stars, like every working stiff,
     have looked us in the eye all this time,

and the sea birds stalled above the surf, wings tipped out
   on the up-draft, have no ontological complaints.
     And so I don't necessarily see the Search

for Extra-Terrestrial Intelligence opposing Social Security,
   but behind me, the Republican estates with driveways
     winding high into the foothills

have me doubting one as much as the other. The sky started out
   as mist, the breath of water heading out after light—
     rain was just an afterthought, a little pity

after a fashion to keep us productive and in place. But it has yet
   to absolve a great indifference to our surroundings.
     Air is all we have to breathe; and the sky,

which we turned into a metaphor, is immaterial, and we have
   let it down—all the clichés apply. Once, I could have
     explained exactly what I stood for. Now,

beyond radiance or repose, a man's not much more than a
   dream on the wind, spray spun up, self-conscious
     residue the sea pays out as it goes. . . .

Looking West from Montecito, Late Afternoon

Beneath hills of agave and eucalyptus,
beneath the Spanish palms and walled estates,
I look across the bird refuge
to East Beach . . . mist in the channel
and only the outline
of the islands floating
vaguely on the blue, just above
the tide and spindrift
choruses of surf.

Half of everyone I've loved
is buried in the cemetery
on the cliff here,
or on the sea out there.
I remember the tangerine trees
just off the road
in Greenworth Place
the overgrown bamboo—
we'd drop our bikes
in the high wild grass and
the clouds would trail us
until we turned home
with the dark.

Now, I think
the gulls and white face coots
have as much of an inner life as I.
The clouds keep pressing.
I have been here 54 years—
I don't know
that I want to go
anywhere else.

Hemingway y yo

> Otherwise, I am destined to be lost, definitively . . .
>
> *—Jorge Luis Borges*

I'm enjoying myself at my local *taqueria*—
authentic colorectal *salsa*, Trio Los Panchos
from the '50s on the Muzak—when
I look up from my *chorizo con huevos*
and catch my reflection in the window. . . .
Looking back at me in a khaki baseball cap
and lion-tamer-rhino-wrestling shirt,
replete with cargo pockets and epaulets,
is a guy in a grizzled beard who looks a hell of a lot
more like Hemingway than Hugh Grant.
Whatever I'd give for a full, frothy mane,
this far into the proceedings, what's the use?
Another year and I'll pass Hemingway
in his last miserable year when he couldn't write,
think, or piss straight against the wall.
I'm telling myself that two out of three's
not so bad—I'm hanging on. My bet is he'd
have traded a bit of bare-knuckle, sun-burned
celebrity, to sit by the lake a little longer now,
penciling in another fish story, covering his head
beneath the stoic clouds, never mind his own
publicity campaign, all the bullets bitten
across the African plains.
                                            Each year I open
In Our Time to that third short inter-chapter
with "young Buckley" coming in with his patrol,
and the German soldiers "potted" as they came over
the wall. World War I, the early battles in Belgium.
I tell my students how I was just a kid, hardly knew him,
and stood to the back, at the edge in the regimental photo—
you can barely tell it's me. And they miss the gag
completely, ask me to bring the picture
into class, look past me, the way they might gaze
at a string of clouds rising over the Apennines
on their summer vacations—dismissing the possibility
of a war ever coming for them.

But I'd go back
in a minute, sit off a rocky point in Cuba on my boat
keeping an eye out for Nazi submarines,
then light the hurricane lamps around Finca Vigía
each evening, a double corona from the Vuelta Abajo,
drinking happily alone this side of the dark.
                                        And why
ever leave Havana, those old soldiers of the Republic
from Spain living in town, that Miro on the wall,
excellent rum on the table, the mail working,
well enough, and down the road a ways, Fidel
perfectly friendly.
                        I'm not going anytime soon
to Sweden to collect a prize . . . but sail fishing
in the gulf, I can still go for that. I have photos
of my stepfather, on a deserted dock off Puerto Vallarta,
a billfish strung up on a rope and pulley,
8 feet into the air, one eye on the sky
like a martyred saint. Frank's young and smiling
in that '40s sepia print, wearing our shirt
and a long billed cap.
                        The government's just announced
it's accepting requests for electronic access to 3,197 documents—
unedited manuscripts, a screenplay for *The Old Man and the Sea*,
insurance binders—kept at the Finca through 1960—
but in the end, nothing that hasn't seen light.
                                        Maybe
I should send a villanelle denouncing Late Capitalism
to Fidel? He might be softened up enough by this point
that he'd invite me for a drink overlooking
the sugar cane, the tobacco leaves of Pinar del Rio,
his memory riding out the last rough swells
out there as far as you can see—not even a beach fire
on the shore, just some barefoot kid
with a weak flashlight looking for a baseball
in the undergrowth.

I won't fly to Miami
for daiquiris or to read my work to the 45 people
in the lecture hall, and why go all the way
to The Algonquin to go a few more rounds with the boys
in bow ties, to see if the acid still rises in your blood
like a toreador's, to see if you can see the horns of time,
the hooking motion ready to blindside you
from the shadows of afternoon? Better finally to sit
in the stands, back of beyond somewhere like Lompoc,
where they wouldn't know Hemingway
from Howard Hughes . . . light up a Montecristo,
the one you're not allowed this month, and settle
for no one, not even God, looking in.

Lost Light

TV signals crawl through the trackless sky,
through the 800 thread-count of the invisible
beams escaping the electric confetti of our ionosphere,

movies and sitcoms representing us
correctly as the violent fools and sentimentalists
we mostly are to whomever tunes in on the far end

and open frequencies of the night where no one
in their cloud-colored bones is slipping through,
though reports maintain the dead are still seen

in linen suits—secret agent Panama hats—at bars
sharing a Singapore Sling with Gene Tierney,
with Ingrid Bergman beneath key lights in Rio,
passing a note to Bob Mitchum in Macao. Yet

according to Air Force spokesmen, none of this
can be confirmed, and despite our satellites
no antecedent for the moon's telephoto
and enigmatic reflection on the bay has been
uncovered. Yet once it was all clear, and I'd never

have guessed I'd come to see how useless it was
to try and think beyond that point in the plot.
Everything, as Marcus Aurelius noted, comes out

of eternity—clouds composed, as are the dreams of men,
of nothing but themselves. . . . Even as a child
I was concerned about what was on the other side

of the high and gauzy screen of air? Each year
we revise our facts, but our essential desires
have never changed. The Chaldeans, versed

in soothsaying and astrology, or Australopithecus,
raising himself on two feet to look up
without the first glimmer of abstract thought,

were gone in a flash on the cosmic story boards—
so much mica dissipating beneath neon marquees. . . .
Nothing's what we make it—but another Christmas,
and I'm tuning in the past again, Bing Crosby
and Marjorie Reynolds in that other world, lost

back there in black & white, where, with just a little
luck, Irving Berlin explains it all—where I came in
after the war, holding onto my mother's hand, in line

on the sidewalk in front of The State Theater, wondering
then as now at the stars—whatever's written up there,
still unreadable, at the grey end of that boulevard of lights. . . .

Drinking Champagne

When he first tasted sparkling wine, Dom Perignon
      imagined he was drinking stars,

bubbles like pearls, rising through liquid the thin
      color of beaten gold . . .

and now, overlooking the sea, the moon dribbling out
      its dabs of light, fingering

the silk trees' old thoughts, I feel it's as close as we are
      likely to come to celestial rewards,

though if I didn't know better in my bones, I'd still
      swear I would be the one

to get out of here alive, the one to forgive the stars
      for misleading us all this time.

Note to Gerald Stern Too Long for the Post Card

No one tells me anything. I don't know
if the juncos in California migrate or not,
and I can't find out on the Internet if we have
the Oregon or the Mexican brand? But like most
birds, I occasionally need to get out of town,
and drove up 101, donating to the oil companies
and stock portfolios for Bush and Cheney's grandkids
as I went—
                    such is the price of a hijacked democracy,
of driving to San Francisco to see friends—all of us now
so far away from where we started out, ragged and reckless
in gas-stingy Volkswagens, ribbons sewn on the cuffs
of our bell-bottomed jeans, sleeping a week or two
on someone's couch between the miserable jobs
of youth.
                    How I got from there to the Fairmont hotel,
even with the discounts, I can't quite figure, talking
aches and organs now, instead of books and the latest
insider trading in New York.
                                        I take a bus
to North Beach and sit at a table outside
Café Puccini with a $3 decaf and listen to the aria
soaring from the counter to the sidewalk
and think how transcendent Pavarotti was—
bless his volume, his beatific register and range—
any god listening would have given him more time. . . .
I never had the chance to hear him live, to rise from my seat
with my soul expanded.
                                        And I was wondering
where in the world your new book was,
and someone who was not Pavarotti was singing
"E Lucevan le Stelle" in the Café Puccini for Christ's sake
as I sat in the shade leaving the red wine alone—
coffee in the big white cup, meatless sandwich,
passing on the cannolis, hoping to buy
more time, intending to get up and down the hills
on my own two feet, with my own short choruses

of breath, the cable cars $5 a pop as they knew
we were coming. . . .   So I walked to that bookstore
off Columbus where everyone's been going since the '50s,
and climbed the stairs where they keep the poetry
and other dangerous materials, and found that tiny dog
rescued on Ninth Street, and the lost poets, and the lost loves—
Thom McCann and the fluoroscope, the amazing bones
of our feet there mid-century, glowing and green
like a bad horror flick.   And when I think of
"Save the Last Dance," I think of The Drifters,
of my high school gym in Santa Barbara, someone
in blue taffeta, or the blameless sea off Santorini,
or my blue surfer Sperry deck shoes—every simple thing
radiating, and the glimmering half-life going out,
except back there, in that amber light. . . .
And I want to know which old love songs, which false-hearted
politicians we should never forget? And why not still curse
the lying sonsofbitches? It's never too late to let out
with something appropriate on all their houses,
to update my list for the top floor in a hotel fire.
Forest fires have burned 3/5ths of the state, and we're all
almost out of water, and my poor pal Gary, evacuated
from his house again—and when it was saved he joked
that he dashed out the door with just my books in his arms,
having thrown all the Krugerrands into his lap-pool
to keep them from melting!   May we all live on air!
I've put in my time practicing, and years worrying,
which is my special talent, along with writing on free post cards
from the Café Puccini, where I keep turning pages
to find the music we've lost, the riffs that keep a little faith
no matter how much finally I don't understand about eternity—
never mind that there are no notices, or announcements,
no travel updates while I am struggling for enlightenment
here in the shade of a tree or two—or that my mother

flew off into whatever ever-after this spring
and just a few fading trills from a spotted towhee
by way of a clue, and the sun again into the sea
without exaltation . . . the only news the hit & run
rhythm of my heart worn down with virus or booze—
the verdict never coming in, just four medications
to outlast whatever it is, to avoid the dual-pronged wires
and industrial-strength device. . . .
                                            And usually,
I'd finish my sandwich, but there are carbohydrates in everything,
and then the concupiscent Italian pastry shop only ten steps
across the street with its nougat and three kinds of cannoli,
though I've mentioned them before, the glorious temptation
and confection of the world—the longing and the lack
of remedy. I leave the crusts on the plate,
there being no blackbirds to befriend, there being no
mind-limbering assistance from a modest glass of Zinfandel
as I read here in the shade—not on assignment, no research
project, just a short vacation, but still trying to dig up
a little background material on the universe
wherever I might find it.
                                    Not a feather of wind
off the Pacific, a high pressure system over
all of California—just the recitative of light
and the bells from Washington Square to amplify
the illuminated dusts sifting down from the high windows
of the hotel with the unlasting fact of our lives—
and the uninformed glory-be of our blood,
and the listening, and the deliberation of the wings.

White Shirt

He had more than one white shirt
                    —*Gerald Stern*

I have bought another one—
                    all cotton,
                                        musty, rumpled
as stratocumulus,
                    and thus sail
                                        into the afternoon
with an armada
                    of grey
                                        uncertain thoughts,
                                                            unaware
as the next one
                    where I am headed,
                                        wrapped loosely
in the garments of wonder.

                    Cloud
                                        by
                                                            cloud
                                                            we arrived
with water vapor
                    draped about our shoulder blades—
the expropriated
                    wherewithal
                                        from the molecular
                                                            blueprints,
the mark-downs and tag-ends
                    indistinguishable from
                                                            the chalk
lines or laundry strings
                    our bilateral lives
                                        spun out from.

Petitioner of likelihoods,
                    apostrophe of dust,
                                        I continue

to take my chances
        at the Thrift,
                prepared for the distance
with its violins,
        evening with its tent
            of fog,
                managing
such luxuries
        in the world—
            any one of us,
                as much as
the next one,
        an orphan
            under stars.

Yet, I'm no closer to being
            finished
                with complaint,
not half way
        ready to wander
            the back lots
                after my last bit part.
I still want something
        after this life
            of second guesses—
every window front display
        going dull as rain . . . .

Beyond the cliff edge
        a patched fabric
            of mist,
              a kite,
skin on a bare frame—
        signs but no
            wonders,
                all that there is

to remember
        behind us.

           Each time I wake,
                  one more version
of myself
      drifts off,
           and I pull on
                another pale and anonymous
standard,
      a flag to represent—
                once the clouds have come for me
and I raise both arms
          to the sky—
             everything I believed in
and have given up.

The Shape of Things

I've been reading the science books again
before bed, where I am lost
in the search for the unified field,
where Einstein said the universe is
curved, where the new cosmologists—
a prolific gang of guessers—un-
characteristically say they just aren't sure . . .
and it's all spinning about
in my drowsy brain, where I look out
the window to the full October moon
above the tomatoes still swelling
on their vines, and it comes to me
that the universe **is** round—
and round, too, whatever
the universe floats in, and
what contains that as well,
ad infinitum . . . .
      Because
belief is circular, day or night,
standing on its hands, turning
cartwheels across the flimsy
infrastructure of the mind, ripples
to the pond edge, around the globe
of the cerebellum that knits the invisible
in place. Because the sky has always been,
and the circulations of the air about us,
and the circumlocutions of every politician,
Sadducee, Pharisee, and Holy Roller,
the men just changing coats
and shipping off over seas to war.

Because whatever we have done
comes back to us, down the causeway
of clouds, the grey circuitry of matter.
Fate as a wheel and the randomness
forever riding there. And the form
of our cells, the protozoa, sea foam,

the soul, and the principle of uncertainty
glowing like cilia all about our skin.
Equally the cranium, the apple forsaken,
the spun planets and flung stars,
the crowns of the beech trees
in sun, and my cats curled up
in every bit of galactic contentment
they will ever know.
                    An atom
is an architecture of worship,
a pint-sized quantum dome—a locus,
a curve satisfying all the points
of the chaotic equation. Because
a photon has a marrow of light,
and a quark and neutrino are infinite
currency, and yet the ineluctable
drift-net of the dark takes it all—
the music of the spheres
sashaying beginning to end,
like *Carmen* for example,
the flaming rose, the flood-lit
stage, the ellipses of love and
the essential accelerant of our blood
as she throws down her cigarette
and circles the men in theme
and variation, like most everything.
Because of the oblong direction
of hope, the spiraled galaxies, our
elliptical desire a case in point,
hard-wired into the stars . . .
and add in, of course, the glorious,
quintessential circumference
of the breast.
                    Because
of the mitochondrial gears,
the distractions of dust
swimming up, of thought likewise

turning to froth, the complete confusion
of our first word with our last,
the apostrophe of breath
that proclaimed us, the little air
we relinquish and absorb.
                              What fits
the hand cannot be gathered
into your arms, into the empty
hoop wishes finally are—
sand dollars and sunflowers,
gold lichen high in the Sierras,
like fragments of falling stars, the 10%
that are iron or nickel, the afterthoughts
and how the ashes are carried
off. . . .
            You can add a zero
to the sum, to the overview,
the intrigues of loss—big bang and
the blue orbs of quasars still bubbling
forth, the unified field gone
to pieces at the get-go,
the blast-furnaces of each recycled
sun spinning in the outer precincts
with our dim expostulations, hoping
to roll it all back into a ball.

Heart Failure

It started at 6 years old—Leslie Baldwin
with her wind-blue eyes, kissing me on the bus,
some instantaneous undoing
in the chest—light rushing out of me
as she held her binder up to block the driver's view,
as I ran around trying to catch my breath,
feeling the clouds rising
as I was unsealed from my bones
a moment, and it all skipped out of time
for the first time then.
                       Soon, I'd never see
her again among dry oak leaves and palms,
a mist through my teens and crazy twenties.
What I thought was something
failing beneath the ribs was nothing
more than the cartilage of desire pulled predictably
out of place. I was one more kid hard-wired
with longing, with some intermittent voltage
through to middle age when everything packed
about my bones began to push the pump overtime,
building up the walls, leaving the gizmo less room
to function, which started to short
the efficient exchange of air and full pulmonary
reciprocation. I never had a chance.

Next thing, I'm standing 3rd from the left
in the 40th reunion photo, all my pals with beta blockers
and ace inhibitors—one friend, with a pig's valve
substituted for his leaky one, didn't make it.
And now I've got a pulsar in my chest
straightening out the electric mumble,
the concertina suck-back and wheeze—
a 60,000 dollar titanium transmitter
with added shock value to set you straight
should the circuitry hit a snafu, the ventricle
spasm for love, loss of blood, or fatigue.
God, some say, gave me this wonky time-keeper—

tin can on a tow rope behind a car
banging along the street in broken rhythm.
What I do know is that beyond the clinic
there are no guardian angels looking into my file.
The virus that inflated my heart
like a bad sausage, like the next thing
to a hand grenade, was just part of the anarchy
of atoms let go to add up, we assume, to something
that makes sense, seems deserved. But philosophy
never filled a cup. The energy of the cosmos
is never lost, only changes form, takes your breath away.
A former student jokes that I'm a Cyborg now,
although everything I love on earth demands
an old school iambic meter to hold us
here, to steady and slow the rotation of the stars
red-shifted, and forever moving away.

Antiques Road Show

On the advice of my urologist, I'm standing, instead of sitting, in front of my
workshop, asking about Jimi Hendrix, who's popped up in a student poem, but no
one has the first idea who he was, not one fuzzy driving bump of bass, or drained,
psychedelic high-note bubbles up from the synaptic mudflats, firing a riff from "All
Along the Watchtower" or "Foxy Lady," there's not one historical nanosecond of
"Purple Haze" flashback to the '60s, and my god, even with music—the lingua franca
of the young—I realize I'm all alone up here, and might as well bring up Bunny
Berigan and "I Can't Get Started" as dear, early-departed Jimi, and when I read the
line from the Veinberg poem in our text about roasting marshmallows with Taras
Bulba on a beach in Carmel, I'm the only one busting a gut, and it's still a half hour
to the break, when I can get down the hall to the Men's room, where I find my-
self thinking about the Trent River, that old bloke fishing off the banks who came
across a rubbish pile with half a dozen paintings he hauled off to the British version
of *Antiques Road Show,* one watercolor of Columbus landing in Hispañiola, and
another of local Cubans in costume, on which the expert used his pointer to trace
the clear signature of Winslow Homer, which a number of folks must have seen and
walked away from asking, "Who's he when he's home?" leaving this enterprising
geezer to be told it's worth 30,000 pounds—100,000 if it were in better nick—and
unlike all those on the show who swear they'll keep it in the family and never sell,
he says he's putting it on the block tomorrow and giving the money to his daughter
for school—no point in keeping it around and letting it grow duller, collecting dust,
like the rest of us.

Poem on a Birthday

The parking garage is full again
except for the top floor,
open to the grey horizon,
to another January day.
I'm downtown to walk around
among the living....
63, and what else is there
but to celebrate the less
than jubilant articulation
of my bones, breathe for all
I'm worth.
                    Yesterday
Margaret Whiting died at 86;
her warm uncomplicated voice
replayed throughout my childhood
with the admonishment
"Beware My Foolish Heart"—
advice I never took....
Mild mannered David Nelson,
of *The Adventures of Ozzie and Harriet*,
lost out to cancer on last night's news,
and just the other day, on the Muzak
in the gas station, Ricky was singing
"Lonesome Town" and "It's Late,"
50 years ago.
                    In the park
off Anacapa Street—where
my mother first took me for walks—
I sit at the picnic table
tracing the initials of the lost
preserved by a green palimpsest
of civic paint. I'm taking notes
with a used Mont Blanc fountain pen
it's taken most my life to afford.
I'm trying to write the truth,
all the other options having vanished
over the hills near Chatsworth

with the dust from the "B" westerns
of my youth.
        When I woke
this morning my great grey cat,
Cecil B., was asleep on my chest,
comforted by the quiet gallop
of the muscle that carries me
day to day—now, spoiled and old,
he sleeps in until he feels me
move with the first grains of light
sifting through, much the way
last evening, I watched
from our balcony
as "Moonlight in Vermont"
floated out the window
like everything in the past
slipping, bit by bit, into the west,
and then I went to bed so that
I might step out early today,
this much closer to the sky. . . .

Metaphysical Poem Ending with That Line from *Dirty Harry*

I've tuned in *Nature* on PBS, a program on the life of Buddha,
and a devotee says reincarnation is like attending junior high school
over and over again . . . but before I go there, there are the Mayans—
who, back in the '50s, in 6th grade Geography, Miss Vasquez told us
invented the 0 and constructed accurate solar calendars, and who
now are grabbing all the headlines with calculations from some
mythical starting point 4,000 years ago which predicts the end
of the world in 2012.
                                    But I didn't catch the date exactly?
Does it keep spinning until New Year's Eve, until the ball drops
with the planet into the black bucket of space? Or is it daily roulette,
everything plummeting all of a sudden like the Dow Jones Industrial Average?
There are 2012 blogs, books, DVDs, YouTube bits, and a B movie
about the rumbling end of everything, a 1970s style Shake & Bake film
with earthquakes and infernos, tsunamis and dust clouds.
                                                      I thought
it was all over in 1962 with the Cuban Missile Crisis, Fidel in his crazy beard
and Khrushchev pounding his shoe. In the school I went to, most of us
quit studying for exams, figuring we wouldn't be there at the end
of the week to take them anyway.
                              And now Clint Eastwood's in his 80s,
his voice more worn with wind and grit than ever. He works out daily
in his home gym, is still trim, tough as beef jerky, but clearly he's fading
away—instead of war, westerns, or rogue cop films, the last movie
he made was about a psychic and the afterlife?
                                          The Syfy channel says
Nostradamus foretold the rise of Hitler and the assassination of Kennedy,
but his coded quatrains make it anyone's guess, anyone, that is,
who can read Tarot cards and the original Old French. I heard nothing
about a Mayan 365-day Vague Year Calendar, any kind of joint
prognostication.
              The Buddha believed that the final outcome
is not significant, but that the understanding of suffering is.
We all have strength enough to endure the misfortunes of others,
La Rochefoucauld told the court of Louis XIV. Buddha preached
that you have to give up everything to gain anything, and, by example,
relinquished his father's kingdom near Kashmir to walk barefoot

on the roads, beg food, and die peaceably amid the dust. Jesus added,
You must lose your life to save it—it's confusing as far back as you go.
If you do the math, figure the odds re the end of days, the probability
of a mystical platform for an afterlife, if you stare up into the indifferent
western sky—a string of enigmatic clouds sauntering across horizons—
and look as far as you are able into the foreseeable future,
You've got to ask yourself one question: "Do I feel lucky?"

Before Long

You must grieve for this right now
you have to feel this sorrow now—
for the world must be loved this much
if you're going to say "I lived"...

—*Nazim Hikmet*

Here's the thing...
4 billion years from now
the Andromeda Galaxy
and the Milky Way
are going to collide.
                    In 2012,
Hubble Space Telescope
researchers concluded
the collision is definite,
and, there's a 50% chance
our solar system will be swept
three times farther out from
the galactic core than it is
today.
            Andromeda has crashed
into at least one other galaxy,
and several dwarf galaxies
are plowing into the Milky Way
right now, but not every star
will collide—
                there are distances. . . .
The analogy comes out to one
ping-pong ball every mile or so—
more integration and stellar drive-by
than obliteration.
                    Either way,
by the time it all bangs up,
all the water on the surface
of the earth will have boiled away
from the increasing luminosity
of the sun, thereby ending
terrestrial life...
                    that's due
in only about 1.4 billion years,

nothing, really, in relation
to the cosmic spread sheet
of time, the algorithm of the dark,
but nothing, finally, all the same . . .
a 1-2-punch for our forthcoming end
the scientists blithely report—
and they're good with that?
                                        I feel
like that character in Woody Allen's
Stardust Memories who obsesses
about the *New York Times* article
on matter decaying, the universe
gradually breaking down and how
there's not going to be anything left—
"Am I the only one that saw that?"
he asks. And though the science is dated
now, that deep sense of urgency
and dread obtains.
                                The great Hikmet,
writing by the Sea of Azov
in the early '60s admonished us
on living—
                        how we must mourn
for the future, or lack thereof,
right now, before the scalded rock
of our planet is released into
the black & white silence of space
without fanfare or a molecule
of moisture left. Last year
the Sea of Azov turned blood-red
near the village of Berdyansk;
older locals warned it was
a sign of coming events.
Hikmet admired the stars,
their winsome, their wondrous
mystery, but he was no

soothsayer, no astrologer;
his rustic soul was rooted
in the soil.
          So what about
the flow chart of light?
And where is Hikmet now,
and where is the dear soul
of my mother? Even the skeptical
don't want to give up thinking
there might be a reservoir
of souls spinning along
with us, mist-like, moon-like,
circling this blue fleck
in the anterooms of the dark.
Even over-compensated
athletes point up to the sky
as if a God were standing
on a terrace of clouds
apportioning lavish rewards
and endorsements for touchdowns
and walk-off home runs, though
they are, as a group, light years from
metaphysicians or cosmologists
who know that there is no "up" out there,
that the galaxies are tilted, tossed out
cattywampus in mostly unfilled space,
only 4 percent of it anything at all
in the Standard Model now.
But for a moment they feel
immortal.
          No way to know.
As a child, I was content
in my little school on the hill
in back of town. I'd race to the swings
and pump my legs, climbing high
into the immediate bowl
of space humming, "Wonderful,

Wonderful Copenhagen, Wonderful
By the Sea"—a song I'd heard
in a movie about a man who wrote
fairy tales for children, and, as I lived
by the sea, which was wonderful
and pure in 1953, it made sense to me,
and for the time being I took the music
and the story on faith, I took the sky,
singing away there, lifting into the air,
mornings and afternoons,
everything then rotating so slowly
about me, so far away, that I was sure
I was a life source as much as
the first stars coming up, though
my feet touched down heading home
each day, firmly, forever on the earth.

Late Iberian Manichaeism & the Crisis of Faith

Castelldefels, 1984

Not the tiniest sleeve
of dust from beneath
the sandals of Christ,
not Santa Lucia's teeth,
or St. Anthony's tongue
on a spike, not even
the certificate of Plenary Indulgence
granted by the Pope
to Rodrigo Diaz de Vivar—
signed over to you
by a minor official
in a dim bodega
in Burgos—will save
the least among us.

There's always someone
with a big idea to sell you,
a grand pay-off down the line—
religion, capitalism, it's the mileage
that does you in. . . .

Believe what you want,
the good, the bad,
the congenitally indifferent
go to the same end
despite the onslaught
of jingles and slogans,
despite the Moors arriving
from the south, or the number
of red-and-white striped pennants
strung up around the parking lot
to trumpet the new refrigerators,
the election of representatives. . . .

Not 100 *Our Fathers*
or 1,000 *Glory Be*s.
It's like a medium priced

Shiraz—fruit forward, a thin finish—
life is front-loaded, so
you might not want to bet everything
on mail-in rebates, on rewards
to come. . . . No flowers, novenas,
or 9 First Fridays, not rib-eyes
given up for Lent,
not a dozen corporal works
of mercy, no lotus blossoms
and rice at the feet of the Buddha
will lift you beyond
the Himalayas, where the last air
surrenders to nothing,
the long, silent volleys of it
expanding all around us. . . .
Plant an olive tree, a lemon,
and someone might
remember you, regardless
of the landscape looking barren
as old bones, the clouds over
Toledo dull as tarnished silverware.
There are no loopholes,
no charge-offs to be taken
as you walk home,
the sunset blinking jaggedly
off the corporate glass
above your head.
              You fall back
on your trees—pittosporum,
podocarpus, and madrone—
planted to encourage the free
exchange of oxygen and CO_2
and the thought that finally
you might be getting somewhere
without owing anything additionally
to the sky, but it's nowhere
near what you'd counted on,

what you were told
would turn up when
you were scraping by
on blood sausage, onions,
and *pan de integral,*
a bleak 80¢ bottle of red
from Penedès. You survived
the summers in Barcelona,
the capital of the Visigoths
where no one stole
the soup money of the poor
on their watch, where you ate
every stale bit of your bread
and ignored the crows
ganged-up on the roof,
resenting the meager offerings
of the air. . . .
                    Each morning
and deep into the night
the heretical mockingbirds
called out demanding a ruling
on the laws of light,
but the commerce of the world
is always only the commerce
of the world. Even as a last resort
now, no one is waiting
for the next visionary
in a white robe to step
from the waves and bring us
another theory about how
our molecules are scattered back
to stardust and recombined
in the unconscious dark
for the benefit of the saints,
about how we are reborn
in the armatures of fire.
Close your eyes—
tell me what you see?

Apnea

They get up on an atom of creation . . .

—*Simon Bolivar*

I'm equipped with a Darth Vader mask
that pumps air down my throat
when the steady traffic of my breath stalls,
blood ballooning in my arteries,
and I jump up gasping in the dark for air,
same way I jerk back into my lane
after drifting on the Fwy, my focus
having slipped beneath a watery haze. . . .
Not enough oxygen, the neurologist says,
delivered to the suburbs of the body—
the brain trying to catch up on Zs
on long commutes, on that soporific
highway along the coast. . . .
                                        The apparatus
reminds me to breathe, reminds me
of the oxygen masks on jet pilots I saw
in the black & white World War II films
at '50s matinees—precious little to take in
in the far cold reaches of the sky.

And I think of masks we wore
skin diving as kids—so called
because we were in our skins,
none of us able to afford wet suits,
just flippers, mask, and snorkel
with which we parsed the kelp beds
and eel grass, disturbing the skates
and sting rays who rose ghostly
from the murky seabed mud.
12 or 13, we could hold our breath
for a minute and a half, sometimes two,
which now sets my wonky heart off
on a dangerous trail in the dark,
leads and gathers like water pulling me
toward a sleep deeper than God's pain.

But each morning now I am more or less
refreshed and walk out back to watch

our hummingbirds whose hearts have
astronomical rates, who have their own ideas
about the franchise of the air . . .
and each evening we watch two or three
strafe and dive bomb the one who
has his beak dipped deep into the feeder,
loading the last sweet propellant,
storing up for the night in thumb-like
nests we never see.
                        And I recall
the newsreels before the double feature
showing the men on Everest bent over
with oxygen tanks and masks
at the roof of the world, and think back
then to 5th grade Geography class
and the misty nothingness like a halo
above Mount Chimborazo in Ecuador,
one degree south of the equator,
the farthest point from the center
of the planet, which is where
the nuns told us we would spend
eternity on a hot rock for our sins,
for fooling around and making faces
when they were facing the blackboard.
Under clear conditions the glaciers
at the summit reflect the sun
and can be seen from the coastal city
of Guayaquil, 140 kilometers away—
a thin atmosphere like the brilliant
haze of dreams. Up there, short of breath,
even Simon Bolivar wrote a poem
about his delirium—coming so near
the unbreathable edge of the Earth—
about being so close, so far removed
from your life you could see the light
exactly where the stars had been.

Creedence Clear Water Metaphysical Reflection

B.A. in English, 21 or 2,
first year teaching Jr. High
and yet not near enough sense
to buy a breadboard, gas-stingy
Volkswagen, to not dump
my first paychecks into a 1969
Plymouth Roadrunner—383 V-8,
Hurst 4-on-the-floor, and all
the ridiculous creature comforts
of bucket seats, white vinyl landau roof,
blue metallic paint, chromed wheels,
and a Craig 8-track stereo tape deck.
Years of comparative deprivation
driving a 1959 rust-bucket Bel Air
covered in Bondo, retreads slick as seals,
had rendered me senseless, left me
with a teenager's glitzy mind-set
measuring happiness in yards of chrome,
in the percolation of Saturday night
radical cams and air inductions revving
in my synapses.
          I drove around
the southland for hours, replaying that title track
from Creedence's *Green River* album,
though I knew that Fogerty had to be
singing about somewhere beyond
the dry river so named in Orange County;
but I couldn't have cared less as it blasted out
the wind wings, as the chassis and every
blood cell shook with a steady rumble,
that muscle car guzzling gas
and glorious time.
          God knew
what I was thinking . . . on the other hand,
since the point, upon reflection, seemed to be
not to do any thinking, I'd have to say

he had no more idea what the hell I was up to
than I did? I was a walking/driving advertisement
for the uselessness and absolute failure
of the long-term positive effects
each and every "steadying influence"
was purported to have on the young . . .
add to that the myth of angels guarding
our direction, helping us make reasonable decisions
in life.
          And though I could get scratch,
burn rubber 1st to 2nd, and 2nd to 3rd,
I was floored when I filled up
at the Atlantic Richfield station,
handing over $8.27 for a tank of ethyl.
That car was, in the long and short run,
a lead-sled—too heavy to pop a wheelie
or beat someone off the line dragging
half a block on State Street as the light
blinked green. But when I stood
on the accelerator, the engine almost jumped
off the motor mounts as I hit the top end
faster than anyone with any sense
should ever want to.
                    One day, stupid-sober
in the afternoon, on an empty back road
in Cathedral City—named, once again,
for God-knows-what, there being no
Cathedral within 90 miles of that sand pit—
I took my college buddies Croal and Vander
for a spin in my new ride. Rolled to a dead stop,
slotted in "Green River," volume cranked
up to 12, revved the V-8 to the red-line
on the tach, and as Fogerty began
to wail at siren volume "Wellllllllll . . . "
I popped the clutch and punched it—
tattooing both my pals with the yank-back

of the seat belts, halfway to whiplash
as I gunned it 3rd to 4th, windows down,
Creedence blaring with that hard-hitting,
high-manic double-twanged driving lead
reinforced with a gut-thumping bass
as we blasted to 85 mph before I eased off,
howling through the roof as if I'd just
established all the evidence we'd
ever need to prove the existence
of the soul—
                    sand and grit flying
in the windows, into our eyes and teeth,
our breath coming up short,
as our sublime collective ignorance
had us smiling away for the whole half mile,
flying through our lives as if we would be
20-something for the next 40 years.

Slow Learner: In the Garden

                    I am a slow study, apparently
nothing for it . . . but I'm happy to be at my lessons,
                    in the particulars, the thorns
or petals, mildew or rust—my doctorate taken in vagary,
                    in staring off at the ivory bells
of yucca in a breeze. I admire clarity, the high, hard edge
                    of oxygen, and yet the formless
beauty, the heady embellishment of orange blossoms—
                    promises that will not apply
in terms of October. The arithmetic of wind—simple plus
                    or minus, everything
blowing away . . . our last warnings in the eucalyptus
                    dry from the air down,
the untranslatable borders, sweet peas on the trellis
                    red and magenta, bruises
dividing the sky. I've come up with next to nothing
                    given the hours spent
observing the plumbago braid itself on air, multiply among
                    the pittosporum and pyracantha.

Now and then I have the good sense to listen to
                    the red sandstone and granite
of the Santa Ynez range, of the San Rafaels, a quiet
                    called for by the insatiable
light from here to Istanbul, where I still see Nazim Hikmet
                    picking an apple in the yard
of that rundown house, in the stuttering poverty of his heart.
                    This place too has run riot
with crab grass and weeds, yet my cat finds a use for most of it
                    while I am trying to abandon
any sense of duty—the jays and mockers, the spotted towhees
                    eager it seems to make up for
my lapses. . . . Meanwhile, the leaves have a language I am close to
                    understanding, and I have a sunflower
volunteering for the sun, and the one representative of bright-faced
                    hope, a new lemon tree
suggesting a democratic splendor, and my neighbor's fig tree

extending over the rain-dulled
fence, and by the time my small transgressions ever get to God,
    should he ever look in this direction,
there will be nothing to be done, our dust dissolving as it does,
    our bodies softening like the figs
I slipped into my shirt pocket and placed on the sill. Do our souls then
    soften as well? It feels as though
they do, although the evidence about us daily suggests they dry out—
    my example is the magnolia leaves
scraping across the patio cement, like crabs with the ancient burden
    of their armor, all that they defy.
Today, I will settle for approximations in favor of certain knowledge
    which has always escaped me,
will content myself waiting for that old hinge in the sky to swing
    open and let a few clouds
float down like blossoms before the white ash and light of time
    go dark for good. I've come this far
with a stone in my shoe, with notebooks half filled, with only
    the corroboration of my doubt,
a little spindrift of belief. The trees saw nothing, the sea turned away
    each evening—the earth spins
slowly and correctly as ever according to Copernicus; the bleached sky
    without a hint. I'll sit here until
I see finally it will do me no good to speculate, to write another word
    about the extravagance of stars.

ACKNOWLEDGMENTS:

from *Dust Light Leaves*

"Why I'm in Favor of a Nuclear Freeze"   *Telescope*
"Dust Light, Leaves"   *Georgia Review*

from *Blue Autumn*

"Halley's Comet from the West Coast, March 22, 1986"   *Indiana Review*
"Evening in Santorini"   *POETRY*

from *Dark Matter*

"Star Journal"   *Passages North*
"Prima Facie"   *Poet Lore*
"Midlife"   *POETRY*

from *Camino Cielo*

"Father, 1952"   *Crazyhorse*
"There & Then"   *Santa Barbara Review*
"The Presocratic, Surfing, Breathing Cosmology Blues ..."   *American Poetry Review*
"Camino Cielo"   *Quarterly West*
"Sycamore Canyon Nocturne"   *POETRY*

from *Fall from Grace*

"Sleep Walk"   *Crazyhorse*
"Opera"   *Iowa Review*
"Vacuum Genesis"   *Kenyon Review*
"Astronomy Lesson: At Café Menorca"   *Quarterly West*
"20 Years of Grant Applications & State College Jobs"   *Quarterly West*

from *Star Apocrypha*

"Early Cosmology"   *Quarterly West*
"March 21st & Spring Begins on Benito Juarez's Birthday
    in Mexico"   *Rattle*
"Photograph of Myself—Monastery of Monte Toro
    Menorca elv. 1.162 ft."   *Mid-American Review*
"Watchful"   *Quarterly West*
"Metaphysical Trees"   *TriQuarterly*

from *SKY*

"To Ernesto Trejo in the Other World"   *LUNA*
"Old News: Poem on a Birthday"   *Poetry International*
"Philosophical Poem on the Usual Subjects"   *Smartish Pace*
"Poem after Lu Yu"   *FIELD*

from *And the Sea*

"Memory"   *Runes*
"Wooden Boats"   *Café Review*
"Loyalty"   *American Poetry Review*
"Travel"   *Denver Quarterly*

from *Rolling the Bones*

"Poverty"   *Five Points*
"We Need Philosophers for This?"   *Cave Wall*
"I Too Am Not a Keeper of Sheep: Variation on a Theme
    by Pessoa"   *American Poetry Review*
"Ode to Clouds"   *New Letters*
"In Memory of the Winos at the Moreton Bay Fig Tree,
    Santa Barbara, CA"   *Cloudbank*
"What Einstein Means to Me"   *Tampa Review*
"Scattering My Mother's Ashes"   *Tampa Review*
"Theory of Life on Other Worlds: Contemplating
    Retirement & Social Security Reform at Shore
    Line Park"   *Prairie Schooner*
"Looking West from Montecito, Late Afternoon"   *Five Points*

from *White Shirt*

"Hemingway y yo"	*New Letters*
"Lost Light"	*Arroyo*
"Drinking Champagne"	*Spectrum*
"Note to Gerald Stern Too Long for the Postcard"	*Blackbird*
"White Shirt"	*Tampa Review*

from *Varieties of Religious Experience*

"The Shape of Things"	*Plume*
"Heart Failure"	*Alligator Juniper*
"Antiques Road Show"	*HUBBUB*
"Poem on a Birthday"	*Rosebud*
"Metaphysical Poem Ending with that Linem from *Dirty Harry*"	*Alligator Juniper*

from *Backroom at the Philosophers' Club*

"Before Long"	*Plume*
"Late Iberian Manichaeism and the Crisis of Faith"	*The Literary Review*
"Apnea"	*ASKEW*
"Creedence Clear Water Metaphysical Reflection"	*Connotations Press*
"Slow Learner: In the Garden"	*Zyzzyva*

Thanks to: Nadya Brown for support and understanding over many years; to my teachers Glover Davis and Diane Wakoski; to Gary Soto for help and encouragement early on; and to Mark Jarman for many years of support and help. For decades of tireless editing and revision suggestions and the unflagging friendship that goes with that, unending thanks to Gary Young and Jon Veinberg. Deep gratitude to Gerald Stern and Peter Everwine for guidance and inspiration and generous support. Finally, profound gratitude to Philip Levine whose poems and generosity gave so many of us our lives in poetry.